CREATIVE AND NON-FICTION WRITING DURING ISOLATION AND CONFINEMENT

This book examines writing that has been created in isolation and confinement, and it explores the stories, characters, and situations that have arisen from these states throughout history. It offers a deeper understanding of how others have found inspiration, purpose, and clarity in these difficult and challenging conditions.

By traversing the narratives of writers, wanderers, mariners, prisoners, recluses, and soldiers, this book offers writers and readers a chance to re-think the parameters of their own circumstances. Exploring a broad range of themes, from writing during a pandemic (COVID-19), travel writing, writing from incarceration, and writing within war and conflict zones, each chapter will look at historical contexts as well as contemporary examples within these themes to demonstrate the rich history and current relevance of writing during confinement and isolation. The book also contains tips and exercises to help develop writing skills during restrictive circumstances.

This is a valuable resource for scholars seeking to observe how writing has developed through various themes of isolation in the past, as well as students at both undergraduate and postgraduate levels of creative writing, communication studies, and journalism seeking to learn through lived experiences how to hone their writing during challenging times.

Ben Stubbs is a senior lecturer in journalism and creative writing at the University of South Australia. He received his PhD from the University of Canberra. Prior to academia, Ben was a feature writer for international publications including the *New York Times* and the *Guardian*. Ben has written three books: *Ticket to Paradise* (2012), *After Dark* (2016), and *The Crow Eaters* (2019). He has also written numerous journal articles and book chapters examining the plurality of travel writing.

CREATIVE AND NON-FICTION WRITING DURING ISOLATION AND CONFINEMENT

Imaginative Travel, Prison, Shipwrecks, Pandemics, and War

Ben Stubbs

Routledge
Taylor & Francis Group
LONDON AND NEW YORK

Cover image: © Getty Images

First published 2022
by Routledge
4 Park Square, Milton Park, Abingdon, Oxon OX14 4RN

and by Routledge
605 Third Avenue, New York, NY 10158

Routledge is an imprint of the Taylor & Francis Group, an informa business

British Library Cataloguing-in-Publication Data
A catalogue record for this book is available from the British Library

Library of Congress Cataloging-in-Publication Data
Names: Stubbs, Ben, author.
Title: Creative and non-fiction writing during isolation and confinement : imaginative travel, prison, shipwrecks, pandemics, and war / Ben Stubbs.
Description: Abingdon, Oxon ; New York : Routledge, 2022. |
Includes bibliographical references and index. |
Identifiers: LCCN 2021059357 (print) | LCCN 2021059358 (ebook) |
ISBN 9781032152509 (hardback) | ISBN 9781032152516 (paperback) |
ISBN 9781003243267 (ebook)
Subjects: LCSH: Authorship--Psychological aspects. | Authorship--History. |
Isolation (Philosophy)
Classification: LCC PN171.P83 S88 2022 (print) | LCC PN171.P83 (ebook) |
DDC 808.02019--dc23/eng/20220214
LC record available at https://lccn.loc.gov/2021059357
LC ebook record available at https://lccn.loc.gov/2021059358

ISBN: 978-1-032-15250-9 (hbk)
ISBN: 978-1-032-15251-6 (pbk)
ISBN: 978-1-003-24326-7 (ebk)

DOI: 10.4324/9781003243267

Typeset in Bembo
by Taylor & Francis Books

CONTENTS

FIGURES

ACKNOWLEDGEMENTS

This book has been a few years in the making. It started as some jotted ideas to help process my inability to travel, though I hope it has resulted in something that not only contextualises our collective COVID-19 experiences, but also contributes to how we might think more deeply about how writing has provided a window for imaginative travel both now and in times of isolation and confinement in the past.

The inspiration for the first chapter came from an article I wrote for *Ethical Space* in early 2019. The meta-analysis of my own journey to Robinson Crusoe Island first appeared in an adapted form within *Text* journal. I thank the editors of both publications for permission to explore these ideas further within this book.

I would like to thank those within UniSA Creative who have supported my writing of this book, in particular Dr Bonita Mason, Associate Professor Sue Joseph, and Professor Susan Luckman for their encouragement. Thank you to Professor Richard Keeble of the University of Lincoln who first saw something in this idea and encouraged me to explore it. Thank you also to Dr Brad West for his advice and guidance during the writing process and to Dr Russell Fewster for telling me all about Sartre's own writing within confinement.

I would also like to thank my family, in particular Laura, Dante, and Franco, with whom I've endured the pandemic and numerous lockdowns during the writing of this book. I may be a little greyer after the experience, though this writing has helped me to see beyond the current predicament as well and to appreciate 'why I write' once again with a sense of clarity I haven't had for a long time.

Ben Stubbs
7 February 2022

1

INTRODUCTION

As the pandemic of our time locked down normal life around the world again and again, the notion of what the future would hold was as milky as a clay cup of Indian street chai. Unsurprisingly, I concluded that I'd never travel again. Even going to the shops to search for toilet paper became an outing worthy of recording.

I had made a career from travel writing where the status of my achievements buoyed me from one journey to the next: seventy countries! Forty-eight hours on an Indian sleeper train! Twenty-four hours awake in Madrid! Once upon a time my travel itineraries for a year might stretch across three continents and my travelling apparel would include hiking boots, anti-malaria medication, SLR camera, maps, and guidebooks. I was quietly chuffed with my worldly ability to say 'If I eat nuts, I'll die' in multiple languages.

As I sat at my desk writing with the standard COVID-19 wardrobe of a two-day old hoodie and slippers, unsure when I would be able to flake the mud from my boots again and start spinning the globe on my desk in anticipation of a new trip, the slow dripping of time started to reveal different layers of my travelling past. At first, I would spend my Saturdays sorting through old travel pictures—of my brother and me on a snowy peak in Kanchenjunga in northeast India, of my wife and me in the Paraguayan jungle or with my children wearing woollen jumpers during a Scottish winter. Then I would start re-reading the travel books that I loved from the past to keep that enthusiasm ticking over—Paul Theroux's train journeys through China in *Riding the Iron Rooster*, Christopher Kremmer's encounters in Kabul rug stores in *The Carpet Wars* and Robyn Davidson's desert sunrises with her camels in the Australian desert in *Tracks*. Still, lockdown continued and my gradual mourning for travel expanded. I would wear the football jersey I bought at a Buenos Aires market and start to question what the point of it all was anyway. So much of travel is rooted in the anticipation of the event, not

DOI: 10.4324/9781003243267-1

the living of the experience: planning the trip, booking the accommodation, organising the route, waiting at the airport, and buying yet another set of universal electricity adaptors before departure, squirming in the plane for 12 hours, arriving at a strange place gripped by jetlag and secretly pining for the familiarities of domestic ritual once the initial buzz of the unfamiliar fades.

And then, one morning, just like the final stage of grief, I began to accept that the notion of travel was different, and it might always be so. During 'the' virus, many of us have become much more well acquainted with our immediate surroundings—I've had more time to ponder the DIY tasks around the house I should complete—the sagging window sash I gaze beyond each day and the sad flower baskets in need of replanting in the courtyard. Alongside this, though, I've realised how much I love the view from my living room, looking out across the misty, winter trees to the Adelaide Hills, and I appreciate the discoveries I've made in my own little plot—which revealed the deeper history of the place I live and the stories existing here beyond my own narrative.

From this moment it became clear that during isolation, while we all experience life behind closed doors during the pandemic of our age, there is an opportunity to look closer and to think more deeply about many things, including the notion of what travel could be in this new world. It made me realise that the 'status' of travel achievements, especially my own, is largely empty unless we remember why we're doing it in the first place. As Karl Stern once wrote, we "seek in the distance what usually lies right in front of us" (cited in Stiegler, 2013, p.48). Perhaps there is some good to come from the pause that COVID-19 has allowed for our travelling selves?

This also poses the question that even though much of the world has realised that travel is 'dead' as of 2020–2022, perhaps it has been a corpse for much longer and we haven't realised it as we tread and re-tread the same tropes, trips and trails again and again?

* * *

"Remember: the importance of elsewhere is predicated upon the preponderance of home" wrote Professor Randy Malamud (2018, p.18) somewhat fortuitously. As a result of the rapid impact of COVID-19, the entire world had to re-think what travel meant as we grappled with life lived from our home offices and kitchen benches. While many cancelled treks to Nepal, put dreams of Venice on hold and wondered what could be substituted for a tropical beach escape at Christmas, it's worth remembering that we're not the first who have had to rethink the concept of travel.

To expand this mourning for travel further, I began to realise that firstly, we certainly weren't the first group of humans to have quarantine imposed on us and to have to rethink the parameters of travel. This has been happening for hundreds of years. Second, I realised that despite these historical lockdowns and bouts of enforced isolation, due to pandemics, personal illness, being shipwrecked, stuck in a trench during a war or locked in a jail cell, people have also found ways to write, and to transport themselves beyond their confinement. Whether it be to make a record of their experience, to find creative inspiration or to simply help them survive the slow passing of each day, there is a precedent for both our inability to travel, and the usefulness of writing in helping us move, both literally and metaphorically, in some cases, beyond our immediate surroundings. The most pressing purpose for this book, written across 2020 and 2021 during my own lockdown in Australia, is to collate and reflect on writing, creativity, isolation, and confinement, and how it might help us think more profoundly about the notion of travel and the boundaries of travel writing as we move beyond COVID-19 and it becomes something that is also written about and reflected on from a distance.

As such, this book acts as not only a response to the isolation of COVID-19 and as an auto-theoretical response that allows consideration of the broader motivations for tourism and travel in the first place, but it acts as a literary journey through time, space, culture and genre to observe and appreciate how others have written about and lived through isolation, as writers wanting to transcend their situations—in both voluntary and involuntary isolation, and how they have travelled, most often symbolically through their isolation. While this might be the first time most of us have experienced seclusion in this manner, my hope is that by observing how, where, and why people have endured isolation and written about the experience, that we might find some perspective and some hope for thinking creatively about our own confinement; and that the various manifestations of desperation, enlightenment, acceptance, madness, and romance might be useful in this context if we write about them.

While the predominant way many people appreciated travel pre-COVID was as a global, wide-reaching, and diverse endeavour, there is now a chance to consider the act of travel from a more humanist perspective. Malamud writes that humanism in this context, "is proximate, intimate, local, contained" (Malamud, 2018, p.6). There is an opportunity here to embrace the humanist constraints of COVID-19 and to appreciate travel anew, where the pre-COVID value of international tourism—worth $1.7 trillion to the global economy (Blackall, 2019)—can be reconsidered for the negative impact this over-tourism also created. With this pause in travel, and travel writing, there is renewed attention on the ethical perception of what we *should* do as travellers, and "further investigation into how we can think about this more imaginatively is required" (Stubbs, 2020, p.11).

While COVID-19 is the most significant period of forced isolation in modern memory, the notion of writing and confinement is nothing new. This book will examine writing that has been borne through isolation. It will explore the stories, characters and situations which have arisen from confinement throughout history, as a way of looking closer, thinking more creatively, and understanding how others have found inspiration, purpose, and clarity while quarantined, when situations might otherwise seem mundane and hopeless. It will also look at what we can learn from these writers about their approaches to confinement, how their styles and psychologies have been influenced by their situations and how their voices have been carried through within their iso-writing.

While the current political environment might seek to diminish creative outputs and relegate writing and creative endeavours well behind those of infrastructure, finance, and industry (Pennington & Eltham, 2021), this book will claim the opposite, that writing is as important now as it has ever been. Writing behind closed doors gives us a reason to keep going, it allows us to impose structure on days without end and it gives us glimmers of hope and fires imaginations that might otherwise diminish. Writing and reading behind closed doors can allow us all to travel in more imaginative ways and to appreciate the journeys we do take with renewed vigour.

Writing within confinement offers both writers and readers a chance to re-think the parameters of 'travel' in their world no matter what the era or the manner of restriction. It did this for Xavier de Maistre who was sentenced to house arrest for six weeks in 1790, and he chose to write a travelogue about the contents his room; it also provides a sturdy rock to cling to for those battling illnesses, both internal and external, which seeks to drag them under—such as Elisabeth Tova Bailey as she documented the tiny world of the snail she discovered beside her bed as she lay in her white-washed apartment for months on end rendered immobile by a neurological pathogen. Writing provides purpose and structure for what exists beyond the walls of confinement, as it did for Australian journalist Peter Greste, as he completed a Masters degree using pencil and paper for his essays as he was imprisoned in Egypt for 400 days. As we all now exist in the shadows of the coronavirus, this is a theme, and an exploration that we all unexpectedly now have a stake in. While the impact of COVID-19 will change over time, the importance of the stories and histories of isolation before now, so we might learn from them, reflect on their impact or gain inspiration, does not.

The chapters in this book examine the themes of travel writing, castaways, incarceration, illness, war and conflict, and writing and COVID-19. Each chapter will look at both the historical context and contemporary examples within these themes to demonstrate the rich history of writing and creativity behind closed doors and the enduring contemporary relevance.

By exploring the narratives of writers, wanderers, mariners, prisoners, recluses, and soldiers, this book will look closely at how writers deal with the obstacles of captivity and how individuals have used writing as a means to explore their own isolation. This collection puts forward the premise that by looking closer and more creatively at the world during these periods, we may find greater navigation for the future and a way we might travel without necessarily leaving the rooms of our confinement.

Beyond the exploration of writers in varied circumstances and how they have approached their isolation, the book will also look theoretically at how these narratives inform our broader understanding of our existence within space. Examples include the analysis and experience of 'vertical' travel, as demonstrated by Alphonse Karr in *Tour Around My Garden* in 1845 as he explored every plant in his garden in

Montmartre with his pet monkey Emmanuel and the emergence of the 'from below' perspective as theorised by Darnton (1984) as an addition to traditional historiography. It will also explore the answers that these writers searched for and discovered as they lived through their confinement, with analyses of the physical, psychological, emotional, and spiritual elements that writers contended with during their captivity.

When we think about it, the act of writing and creating nearly always happens behind closed doors, though the main element here for most of us is choice. We choose to close the office door or retreat to the quiet bedroom to write. All of a sudden the notion of not having a sense of choice and being thrust into a set of circumstances and a solitary world is something that all of us have in common, something we maybe couldn't fathom before all this. This could be the most extreme form of incarceration, the musings of a travel writer in his room, or someone finding joy in their world from the confines of their sick bed, though what is clear is that writing in isolation is nothing new, and suddenly it is something we can relate to.

So, while we all appreciate the notion of being behind closed doors in a manner none of us could have predicted or chosen, the opportunity to consider the creative significance of this as proximate travellers is more telling than ever.

References

Blackall, M (2019). Global tourism hits record high, but who goes where on holiday? *Guardian*, 19 July. Retrieved from www.theguardian.com/news/2019/jul/01/global-tourism-hits-record-highs-but-who-goes-where-on-holiday (accessed 22 October 2020).

Darnton, R (1984). *The Great Cat Massacre and Other Episodes in French Cultural History*. Basic Books.

Malamud, R (2018). *The Importance of Elsewhere: The Globalist, Humanist Tourist*. Intellect Books.

Pennington, A & Eltham, B (2021). *Creativity in Crisis: Rebooting Australia's Arts and Entertainment Sector after COVID*. Centre for Future Work and the Australia Institute. Retrieved from https://australiainstitute.org.au/wp-content/uploads/2021/07/Creativity_in_Crisis-_Rebooting_Australias_Arts___Entertainment_Sector_-_FINAL_-_26_July.pdf.

Stiegler, B (2013). *Traveling in Place: A History of Armchair Travel* (trans. P Filkins). University of Chicago Press.

Stubbs, B (2020). Close travel: On the ethics of writing about the near-at-hand. *Ethical Space Journal*, 17(3), 11–17.

2

TRAVEL WRITING

While conventional travel was curtailed in 2020 and 2021 as we became more well acquainted with our significant others' habits than we ever thought possible, there is a precedent for thinking about journeys and how they are written about in a more imaginative sense—travel and the near-at-hand.

From this prompt comes the notion of 'close travel' a mode of looking around us and within our environments more thoroughly before venturing across the globe in search of adventure, encounters with the 'other' and cultural immersion far from the places we call home.

This pause in our ability to travel also allows for a re-thinking of the increasing irrelevance of traditional travel writing. Not only has the world been thoroughly explored, the historical hangover of imperialism, orientalism, and capitalism has left travel writing as a poorly regarded cousin of journalism. The imposition of COVID-19, where travel has been largely impossible, could be said to have sped up the inevitable death of the form. Curiously, though, this is where a focus on close travel, which is essentially travelling without travelling, could be the saviour of the genre. It affords a re-focusing, a new opportunity for narrators and a chance to look closer in a manner that has not been considered, at least as its central concern, before now.

This idea of more 'vertical' travel and travel writing where we immerse in the spaces around us in greater detail, peeling back layers of history, botany and culture is not something that has appeared as a result of the current virus either, it goes back to the late 18th century in Turin and a man named Xavier de Maistre.

De Maistre was a young army officer and aristocrat who was caught fighting a duel in the early years of the French Revolution. It's not known what happened to his opponent, though for his trouble de Maistre was sentenced to six weeks of house arrest in his bedroom in Turin's citadel in 1790. De Maistre's brother was the political philosopher, moralist, and diplomat Joseph de Maistre and they had

DOI: 10.4324/9781003243267-2

travelled together a great deal before Xavier's arrest. Rather than sulk through his imprisonment, Xavier decided to challenge the popularity of the imperialist travel writing of the era and he wrote a travel book about the contents of his bedroom. De Maistre wrote *A Journey around My Room* while being kept behind the closed door of his own chamber, with only his valet who would deliver his meals, and his dog, Rosine, for company. De Maistre observed his surroundings through a different lens, detaching and looking with new eyes to give the reader an alternative perspective on what travelling could mean:

> What a comfort this new mode will be to the sick; they need not fear bleak winds or change of weather. And what a thing, too, it will be for cowards; they will be safe from pitfalls and quagmires. Thousands who hitherto did not dare, others who were not able, and others to whom it never occurred to think of such a thing as going on a journey, will make up their minds to follow my example.
>
> *(De Maistre 2017 [1794], p.4)*

De Maistre's room became a place with latitude and topography, "I will be crossing it frequently lengthwise, or else diagonally, without any rule or method" (ibid., p.7) he remarked. De Maistre immersed in the scenes of the paintings on his walls and saw his bed as a vehicle for imaginative transportation with Rosine. De Maistre described the positioning of his bed as he would a street scene in Paris or the arrival to a new city, "Once you've left my armchair, walking towards the north, you come into view of my bed, which is placed at the far end of my room: it's a most agreeable sight" (ibid., p.8). He writes how the bed catches "the first rays of the sun" which play upon the curtains and of the patterns the shadows of the elm trees leave on his wall. It is the place that "witnesses our birth and death; it is the unvarying theatre in which the human race acts out, successively, captivating dramas, laughable farces and dreadful tragedies. It is a cradle bedecked with flowers; it is the throne of love; it is a sepulchre" (ibid., p.9).

De Maistre often addressed the reader directly and was unapologetic for including so many details in his exploration. He includes a chapter on his memories of the engraving on his wall, giving the reader a description of what they would see if they were sitting on the bed next to him: of the image of an unhappy Charlotte with trembling hands, cleaning Albert's pistols, with a melancholy look on her face of inconsolable love imprinted on her features.

De Maistre writes of the stories behind his preference for rose and white coloured furniture, of his need to don proper travel clothes—namely his favourite winter travelling jacket—every day of his incarceration and his undying affection for his dog, "when you set off to climb Mount Blanc, or when you go to visit the wide open tomb of Empedocles, you never fail to describe the smallest details precisely" he writes of the imperialist travel writing fascination for the most boring minutia, of the "number of people, the number of mules, the quality of the provisions, the excellent appetite of the travellers—everything, in short, up to and

FIGURE 2.1. Xavier de Maistre travelling in his room
Source: public domain, Wikimedia commons

including the times your mounts stumble" and as such de Maistre promises his readers that he will "devote an entire chapter" (de Maistre 2017 [1794], p.24) to his beloved dog Rosine.

There was important truth in de Maistre's assertion as much of the world was gripped by the travel adventures and Burton-esque conquests of far-off lands and the lengthy descriptions of hills and marshes. Even from an Australian point of view, with the great travel exploration of the 19th century as Burke and Wills scrapped to the top end of Australia in the name of expansion, much of the writing of their initial narrative is concerned with the preparations and accoutrements of their journey as they set off from Melbourne in 1860 with 26 camels, 23 horses, 19 men, six wagons and 270 litres of rum. As such, de Maistre informs the reader, that using the same principle he will make his companion, who is the most importance presence in his life, central to his travel narrative.

De Maistre was so taken by the journey that he subsequently wrote *A nocturnal expedition around my room* in 1825 to revisit the country which he had travelled through with so much enthusiasm previously to further push the boundaries of the form by concentrating only on the night-time perspective of his travel narrative within his room. Here de Maistre revisits his favourite destination so readers can appreciate the view across Turin to the other apartments in darkness and to share with him his thoughts on love and loneliness while imagining what those people inhabiting the windows and terraces across from him might be doing during the night.

Beyond the vertical attention, de Maistre's writing allowed an inner focus and reflection that the adventure travel of the era did not acknowledge, "not only did I succeed in forgetting my past, but I was even able to look my present troubles in the face" (de Maistre 2017 [1794], p.133). He writes at the conclusion of his incarceration of the benefits of slowing down and looking closer. There were many writers who were inspired by this new style, and there were numerous poor imitations of de Maistre's provocative and enthusiastic re-focusing of travel by unheralded and anonymous writers, with titles such as *My Cousin's Journey around His Room, Journey around My Cellar*, and *Journey around My Pockets* which, perhaps unsurprisingly, did not see the same success as de Maistre's work.

While de Maistre's writing, and even the enthusiasm with which he embraces his task might seem at odds with 21st century living, and especially the caution and apathy we find ourselves experiencing during COVID-19, there is something about this positive mindset worth reflecting on further. One thing the pandemic has done is to demonstrate the shared experiences between billions of people, who previously had little in common collectively. We're all dealing with isolation, uncertainty and a fogginess for the future which binds us. What we can learn from de Maistre's donning of travel jackets and journeys on his bed is that thinking deeper about what we want from travel, whether that's an absence of responsibility, a cocktail before midday or the chance to immerse in something unfamiliar, is important. It also highlights how we can achieve many of these things without needing to engage with cruise ships, trips costing thousands of dollars or travel practices that might be ethically and environmentally questionable. While I haven't taken to journeys around my bedroom, what I have done is to take care to maintain my own children's enthusiasm for the outside world—as adults we might understand that travel will continue in one way or another in the future, though it's a bigger proposition for a 9-year-old and a 7-year-old who are suddenly presented with a world of hand sanitiser, face masks and social distancing footprint outlines on the floor of every place we visit. With this in mind we cook foods from different countries to expand the reach of our kitchen—aloo gobi one night and empanadas the next, we spin the globe and investigate the countries our fingers land on and even if all they learn is how to swear and ask for chocolate milkshakes in the Argentinean Spanish of their grandmother, it keeps the notion of travel present, even when the ability to 'go' is not.

Notions of the vertical

In her essay on localising Italian travel writing, Joanne Lee sees close travel as a way for writers to attempt to "uncover hidden aspects of familiar places, often their native town or region" (Lee, 2012, p.203). Lee cites the travel writing of Italy as an example of this, where the focus previously has been on the writings of Anglo-Americans which has, in turn, shaped the way that both outsiders and Italians view themselves. Today, domestic writers are better able to capture the essence of Italian "localities, regions, towns and cities" (ibid., p.204), she argues.

This notion of close travel has also been broadly identified by Michael Cronin as 'vertical travel':

> the temporary dwelling in a location for a period of time where the traveller begins to travel down into the particulars of place either in space (botany, studies of micro-climate, exhaustive exploration of local landscape) or in time (local history, archaeology, folklore).
>
> *(Cronin, 2000, p.19)*

Cronin examines the two different modes of travel—deep or cursory—as he labels them and finds commonality with our understanding of language as we travel. For Cronin, cursory language is that which we interpret in our everyday lives on a surface level, whereas a deep understanding of language relates to the sub-languages we are exposed to while travelling in a slower and more vertical sense. This includes slang, abbreviations, and regional dialects. Cronin gives the example of the 'horizontal voyage' into and across a foreign country not being a substitute for the 'vertical' understanding of its culture, customs, slang and formalities—where simple exchanges such as dining at a foreign restaurant seem perplexing and strange.

Alasdair Pettinger writes in *Key Words for Travel Writing Studies* (2019) that it is not so much a literal re-thinking of the travel within travel writing (as in Robert Macfarlane's *Underland* where the author goes beneath the surface of the earth for his exploration) but a more thoughtful and introspective deceleration focusing on the depth of the experience. This does not suggest that all manifestations of this form of travel writing should be philosophical rather than geographical in nature either. Pettinger writes that this form of introspective travel may have its roots in the fieldwork nature of modern anthropology, where the intensive focus on small communities was given preference and anthropologists practised 'thick description', as Clifford Geertz called it (cited in Pettinger 2019, p.278).

This rediscovery of seemingly mundane or overlooked places is at the centre of both Cronin's and Pettinger's interpretations of the vertical rather than the horizontal and more conventionally tourism-oriented journey. Charles Forsdick (2019) highlights the importance of the writer's relationship with space within their writing so that they can more readily embrace the awareness of everyday occurrences as vertical travellers.

This new notion of rethinking space and valuing the mundane as an ethical and creative choice, acts as a counter to the previously assumed notion of the importance of distance and the predominance of the surface experiences of many travel writers from the 18th and 19th centuries. This type of travel writer was labelled by Mary Louise Pratt as the "monarch of-all-I-survey" trope where the travel writer strived to obtain a more omniscient view of their location, from a more elevated and "above the subject" position, rather than preferring a closer and more engaged station. As an example of this "vivid imperial rhetoric" (Pratt, 2002, p.202) Pratt cites Richard Burton in *Lake Regions of Central Africa* (1860) as a prime example of this all-conquering, postcolonial perspective, where Burton vies to 'win' these locales for the mother country, and he over-dramatises the discovery and description of mundane places as exotic and momentous.

It is the 'geometry' of the journey rather than the geography which is the most important consideration with vertical travel writing, irrespective of the literal or metaphoric focus. Forsdick uses the example of concentric circles to explain the geometry of travel to divide up and expand focus within vertical writing more slowly and methodically, "Vertical travel reflects the experimental potential of travel writing to propose new and often defamiliarising ways of viewing and engaging with elsewhere" (Forsdick, 2019, p.101).

Stiegler writes that of all the room travel presented in the era of de Maistre, it offered comfort and a chance to appreciate the richness around us, "Such an expedition is not one into strange lands but rather one into the strangeness of the familiar" (Stiegler, 2013, p.2).

Venturing just beyond the bedroom, there were also many notable nature focused travel narratives to further expand the point of view. In the 19th century, Heinrich Seidel refocused his apartment into a microcosm, where each item had a history and an interconnected story, Gaston Chaumonts wrote *Journey to My Window* focusing on what lay directly outside his home, drawing on the interior of the room and the reflection of the framed world outside it. Similarly, Alphonse Karr in his *Tour round My Garden* produced two volumes and seven hundred pages focused solely on his garden where he lived in Montmartre with his pet monkey Emmanuel.

Alphonse Karr was a bourgeois eccentric of French literature. According to his friend Walter Benjamin, he lived in a sparse, black, one room apartment with windowpanes of violet and white frosted glass. It was devoid of furniture and Karr would sit on the floor to write. This wasn't an issue for Karr though, as the space that captivated his attention was the apartment's garden, complete with herbarium and a small grotto with its own fountain.

As such, Karr's garden becomes his entire world. In his book he describes nothing more, but nothing less than his garden. The narrative is presented as a series of diary entries as if being written to a friend who is off on a more 'traditional' voyage around the world. He writes:

> I've never really understood the traveler's concerns. I've never found anything in another country that you couldn't find in the same form right in your street. Many people have gone to America to look at trees, or travelled to China to discover new people. The only excuse the traveler has for going so far away in order to see what's right outside his window is that one cannot lie about what is visible to everyone else.
>
> *(Karr, 1845, p.18)*

There is an important conclusion to be drawn from Karr's writing. When we look at the travel narratives of the era—of adventurers bringing back stories that were hardly believable, where the line between the real and the embellished account was impossible to know, the concrete evidence of Karr's garden is irrefutable and reassuring.

Karr travels plant by plant through his garden and writes as if sending back dispatches from a far-off mythical land. "I go down three steps. Here we are in China!" (Karr, 1845, p.18) he writes as he encounters a Chinese wisteria, bringing the far near as a result. He writes of the 5-month journey of a gall wasp across a leaf, a bee flying past with its feet sticky with yellow stamen dust, and how when a plant dies, it disturbs an entire realm of other living things. It is a story of the re-enchantment of the world and could be seen as an original *Private Life of Plants* long before Sir David Attenborough attempted it.

Karr writes with the same passion we might expect from a traveller on their first ascent of Mount Everest. While the book might sound like an over enthusiastic catalogue of flora and fauna in painstaking detail, it is the depth that this wandering allows that gives Karr's close travel its real value. He writes of the immense cycles of nature as entire ecosystems perish, rose petals enclose beetles, tiger lilies drop fronds, and the sun sinks below the clouds submerging their resident insects and parasitic attachments along with them:

> Seriously this fiction, which poets good and bad have all abused, of showing that trees and flowers partake our sadness and mourning, our joy and our pleasure, is, for me, a less elevated poetry than the superb indifference of nature.
>
> *(Karr, 1845, p.262)*

Karr concludes his narrative by bringing the juxtaposition together, as the 'traveller' he has been writing dispatches to returns, thus also reflecting the depth of his journey and the energy he has gained from this different, stationary mindset, rather than expelled like his counterpart.

> I was just at this point of my journey, my good friend, when an unusual noise interrupted the wonted silence of my retreat. It was the noise of a carriage and the horses galloping, with the crack of the post-boy's whip. It was you, returned from your long voyage before I have half-finished mine. But you could only afford me a few minutes.
>
> *(Karr, 1845, p.262)*

Karr's writing highlights where we can look closer at the world with a sense of positivity around the impact of the pandemic of 2020–2022. In Margaret Simons's June 2020 article in *The Saturday Paper* she writes with poetic observation of her garden and its importance to her life during isolation, of sprouting bulbs, marigolds, and wriggling worms:

> Every morning, after first coffee, I do what I jokingly call my tour of the grounds—a three-minute journey from rear fence to front strip. It begins with using an old soft-drink bottle to water the mushroom farm that I keep just inside the back door, next to the vacuum cleaner.
>
> *(Simons, 2020)*

As I began to venture out from my home gradually during the first lockdown, the most frequented shop outside of the supermarket for essential items was undoubtedly the hardware store. As people have been forced to look at their gardens and patios and pot plants for weeks on end, the prompting of presenters on *Gardening Australia* seems to have spread like the weeds so many of us now notice. Whether it's planting herbs on your veranda to add to homemade salads, or preparing patches of your garden for spring daffodils, the fascination with each individual plant and the significance of the space around us is something many of us now have time to consider.

Inspired by Karr's positivity and perseverance I too tried to spend extended time out in my garden to look closer—to pass the time, but also to understand what Karr was doing. The way I could appreciate my garden more vertically was by segmenting it into senses. On a misty Monday I began with the smells of my garden. In the dark soil by the fence, the sharp stench of onion weeds leaked across the garden as I inspected their buried bulbs. Further along in the hanging baskets the thick, sweet smell of the geraniums clung to my fingers like the cloying perfume of an elderly aunt. My favourite aroma from my garden, though, was from the big, gnarled peppercorn tree in my front yard. I grabbed a handful of pods and rubbed them along my palms—the spice that hung in the air transported me momentarily to the same tree on my grandparent's farm when I was a kid. Later in the week I focused on the sounds of my garden. This required me to stop and slow down. I heard the rustling of black birds in the undergrowth as they look for grubs. In the afternoon, as the wind picked up, I heard the limbs on the stand of gum trees across the road with their hollow whistle as they shook with each gust. As I sat on the backstep, I realised that this refocusing has displaced concerns for my work emails, my next Zoom meeting and everything else momentarily. As the sun appeared from behind a cloud, crunching in the tangle of grapevines below me revealed a baby blue-tongued lizard venturing out onto the steps to soak in the sun; the blue, purple and grey scales on its back shimmering as they caught the light.

This notion of looking closer is something that has been encroaching on my own practice as a travel writer in the time leading up to COVID-19 as well. As I sought to understand my home with more depth, it occurred to me that in all my career, I had always looked outwards and the realities of where I lived, in the state of South Australia, were largely a mystery as I had endeavoured to tell stories external to my everyday life. The value, as a traveller, of getting to know the layers of the place you live in greater detail were also part of what I taught my students in our Creative Writing Theory and Practice course. Just because the small city of Adelaide may seem mundane to us, as we live in it and experience it every day, the notion of a city full of parks, verdant hills behind it and then a 1 million km^2 state with deserts, the oldest mosque in Australia, hidden caves with megafauna skeletons, nuclear blast testing zones from the 1950s and enormous rivers once full of paddle steamers is exotic and unusual to many.

Taking my own advice somewhat, during a weekend of gardening before the pandemic I uncovered a series of old brick fragments buried in the clay soil of the garden: "The history of this place was in my hands, hiding just beneath the soil. I pulled up a curved lip of clay of from beneath a tangle of old roots and wriggling worms; it was the edge of a brick" (Stubbs, 2019, p.6).

As more and more shards surfaced, it made me curious that there was another story buried beneath the surface of this place I assumed I knew so well and it led to the writing of my book *The Crow Eaters*. The bricks prompted me to investigate the stories of the town I live in at the local library. The village I live in, Littlehampton, was more than the busy road and the service station I now associate it with. It once had a brewery, a railway station, a tannery, and a vibrant community. It also had two brickworks, including the smokestacks of the Coppin Brothers brickworks dating back to 1850 on the spot where my house now sits:

> Many years have passed since Coppin Brothers closed down. Before my family arrived here, an old lady who lived in a cottage surrounded by overgrown gardens and blue painted walls owned our block. Within her overgrown gardens the history of the brickworks and the story of my street was gradually swallowed by soil and tree roots.
>
> *(Stubbs, 2019, p.6)*

This discovery highlighted for me the value in looking closer, and even if the bricks or the village story isn't where we end up in our own close travel, it is a new place to start. This is also something I've noticed with the incorporation of important Indigenous stories forming a much more significant part of the layers of travel narratives in Australia. There is now an acknowledgement of the different Aboriginal nations, the different language groups and the intricate stories of Dreaming and Indigenous astrology which add depth to our understanding of place once we focus more readily on the near-at-hand and the layers of story around us.

* * *

As part of the exploration of travel in isolation it is important to note the imbalance between male and female contributions to travel writing historically, as the status of women was often deemed less important and the impediments to travel were much more obvious for women, despite the fact that women travel writers, especially during the Romantic era, were "receptive to the many passing impressions that they saw on their travels, which gave them a keener sense of the singularities of the environment around them" than their male counterparts, writes Martin (2008, p.39).

As such, another less obvious interpretation of travel, writing and isolation comes from the Frauenzimmer, a German word meaning a wood or timber chamber for women—a parlour where women work, congregate or gather. The Frauenzimmer also refers to those who congregate within it. The complexity of this type of room is not to be understated, and as with many representations of gender in this era, when male travel writers could travel and conquer places that were to be hardly believed, there was a sanctuary and secrecy to the Frauenzimmer, and the room travel writing that occurred within it that gave it the same introspection and wonder as seen through Karr and de Maistre's journeys. In Annegret Pelz's *Journey Through My Own Strange Land* she writes of Sophie La Roche in 1799, who was one of the first female writers to travel through her own interior space. This is not about the inner life of the narrator, but the perspective of one who captures the narrative and importance of a traveller's sense of space in an era when travel was both socially and culturally constrained for the female traveller. As La Roche looks closer at her space, and thus alienates from its familiarity, it becomes the external manifestation of her inner thoughts, allowing more objective travel through it. La Roche was well travelled in the traditional sense, though on one planned trip to Italy she was unable to take due to the death of her young son, she retreated to her room and wrote an imaginary journey of this voyage while never leaving her desk to fulfil the request of her son who found her writing space, with the desk, books, and travel pictures so captivating. Part of her reconciling the death of her son was by getting to know, and writing the intimate details of, the objects in her room—each book and paper on her desk and on her shelves act as an "auto-geography" (cited in Stiegler, 2013, p.35) to transport this space beyond its four walls.

Looking differently at close travel

This realisation of the depth of room travel is something particularly relevant when also considered alongside the impact of COVID on the tourism sector. As the cruise industry scrambles for relevance in the wake of mass infections, shutdowns and the stories of cruise ships floating offshore and between ports with stranded international crews, it is worth remembering that for all the current negative connotations, the idea of travelling 'with' a room is something which has particular relevance for cruise passengers.

While there are many extensions of the notion of close travel, one that has had a lasting impact on modern tourism and travel writing, and has become increasingly relevant in the COVID era, is the vertical travel of Mark Twain—the journalist and celebrated author of *The Adventures of Tom Sawyer* (1876) and *The Adventures of Huckleberry Finn* (1884). Twain became the first cruise travel writer when, in 1867, he took the *Quaker City* steamship from New York to Europe and the Holy Land with a ship full of American tourists for company. "It was a novelty in the way of excursions—it's like had never been thought of before, and it compelled that interest which attractive novelties always command" (Twain, 2010 [1869], p.19). This is the first example in modern travel writing where the mode of transport becomes not only part of the pleasure of the trip but also a key part of the story. Twain's resulting book, *The Innocents Abroad*, originally published in 1869, became the best-selling travel book of the century and Twain's most popular book. "They were to scamper about the decks by day, filling the ship with shouts and laughter—or read novels and poetry in the shade of the smokestacks, or watch the jellyfish and the nautilus over the side" (Twain, 2010 [1869], p.19). Twain writes of his companions on their voyage. While the shore excursions (and Twain's lampooning of his fellow passengers and those they encounter along the way) is a large part of the story, the close travel perspective of the *Quaker City* and the experiences onboard are ever present throughout the narrative.

Twain's cruise writing also precipitated some of the first 'travelling with a room'—and the introduction of caravan travel writing in the early 20th century. While the room travel of de Maistre allowed for a concentration on the vertical possibilities of travel, the broader idea of room travel is one which is worth further attention.

Throughout history it's been simultaneously known as the 'Prairie Schooner', 'Overlander', 'Winnebago', 'Wagoneer', 'Landyacht', and 'Terra Cruiser', though the humble caravan is also a peculiar and important aspect of the history of close travel. While the caravan might be ever-present in the tourism landscape of tourist parks and grey nomads, it has a close relationship with vertical travel and the enigmatic French literature avant-garde. Raymond Roussel, who counted Foucault, Leiris and Breton as his peers, had his own Roulotte built in 1925—a nine-metre-long van that would allow him to visit the Pope (and Mussolini) in his purpose-built car. It is telling that despite Roussel's eccentric journey, almost 2000 verses of his *La Vue* are devoted to the descriptions of the view of the inside of his trailer—of the ornate double bed, the deep bath, the fireplace and sitting room included. Roussel became notable for travelling without travelling. He visited India, Australia, New Zealand, the Pacific archipelagos, China, Japan, and America, yet in his own words the only observations he took from these places were from his own books, as he would spend days on end with curtains drawn working in his cabin—on boats, trains or his touring car as he was transported into his imagination rather than the surface views out his windows. As Michele Leiris noted of his eccentric methods, Roussel travelled across the world without the need to leave his room at all (Leiris, 1984).

While domestic ritual as a travel theory is focused on the tasks performed in the house to maintain continuity, the escape from this, for both men and women, is often seen as the main motivator for travelling—to escape this domestic rhythm. Despite this, there are three elements of travel and domestic ritual which often see the recreation of these rituals: through the artefacts we bring with us to recreate home, the rituals we embody while travelling which reflect home and the way these ideas of home are written about. For Sarah Murray in the late 18th century, she brought together the strands of domestic ritual and travelling with a room in one journey as a way of forging identity through isolation.

In 1796, Murray, a 52-year-old widow, departed London with a maid and manservant in a customised carriage to explore the far reaches of Scotland to write a guidebook on her five-month journey. This not only challenged the typical male grandiose expeditions of the time, but it also revealed an interesting version of room travel as an inclusion in her exploration in what was only the second printed guide to Scotland and an adventurous and practical guide aimed at women of similar class and station. She also travelled alone (aside from her servants) which in this era was a rare and bold acknowledgement of isolation which made her both an ordinary and extraordinary traveller of the era.

As Murray travelled the Scottish Highlands before the advent of tourist infrastructure, she established a list of necessary items for gaining control over the isolation of her environment. Murray created a home in her carriage as she travelled:

> the side next to the travellers should fall down by hinges, at the height of their knees, to form a table on their laps; the part of the box below the hinges should be divided into holes for wine bottles, to stand upright in. The part above the bottles, to hold tea, sugar, bread, and meat; a tumbler glass, knife and fork, and salt-cellar, with two or three napkins: the box to have a very good lock. I would also advise to be taken, bed-linen, and half a dozen towels at least, a blanket, thin quilt, and two pillows; these articles will set a traveller quite at ease.
>
> *(Murray, 1982 [1799], pp.39–40)*

Murray re-created a travelling 'home' inside the carriage, decked out to permit her to continue living with the etiquette and expectations of her upper-class London home and to create a space away from both the landscape and the people of Scotland.

This inverted notion of travel, looking at travel with a room and the idea of creating a home as we venture across the globe is something that is part of the contemporary notion of travel and isolation as well. Grey nomads, particularly in Australia, are sometimes looked at with scorn for their homogenous packs travelling through the country while facing inwards, rather than appreciating the diversity of the country beyond their awnings. However, this grouping of the more than 200,000 grey nomad journeys through Australia is a generalisation, one I was guilty of myself before I began to think about it in the context of the pandemic. As Onyx and Leonard write of the motivations of many caravaners, "People choose, create, and at times revise their life stories" (Onyx & Leonard, 2007, p.382) and this idea of travelling with a room is particularly relevant now.

The practice of hitching a caravan and going on a journey for leisure dates to 19th century England and the Romani and Gypsy people who would travel between places with a trailer or caravan set up for sleeping, eating and communal living around the 1860s. Before this, caravans were part of travelling circuses throughout England in the 1820s. The history of this travel with a room goes back much further, however. Lee (1974) cites the Tartars of the 13th century who would travel with a tent on wheels and later the purpose-built shepherd's hut on wheels of the 14th century which is now detailed in the British Museum. While nowadays caravans regularly contain satellite dishes and solar panels, the opulence of room travel dates back to the Earl of Peterborough who travelled in a caravan in the 18th century complete with a full kitchen, four bedrooms and a dining table to seat six. Later, in 1787 Catherine the Great's caravan needed 16 horses to drag the jewel encrusted chamber across the Crimea. The fairest caravan of them all, though, would possibly fall to Napoleon, whose campaign caravan contained chambers for sleeping, eating, washing, cooking, strategy rooms and map reading chambers. It was appointed in gold and silver with mahogany cutlery boxes and a built-in chamber pot before it was captured at Waterloo.

The emergence of the caravan allowed for extravagant close travel as the nobility in Europe ventured out into the world. The Duke of Newcastle had a caravan built that contained an open fireplace, armchairs, a wine cellar and space for two built-in bird cages.

In Australia, caravanning as a leisure activity dates to the 1920s and it is now worth $2.3 billion to the tourist economy (Carruthers, 2020). While I was initially dismissive of this form of insular travel, I was proved wrong as a friend invited me into his own travelling room. It wasn't about being insular and restrictive, the caravan was a 'place' in itself. Yes, it was full of things: diesel heaters, fridges, and TVs to make the journey comfortable, but it was like being let into his home. The caravan was full of stories and intimacy—people they'd met, weekends they'd shared with family as pandemic restrictions lessened, and possibilities for the future as they embraced the new order of how the whole world may have to travel in the future and planned for adventures with their children.

The rethinking of the 'intra-tourist' gaze, where tourists and travellers of all sorts are aware of each other's presence in place and act as a more aware and engaged presence in place is something which I think encapsulates the hopeful view of the future of travel, which might be closer than many of us realised.

Room travel and fiction

While Xavier de Maistre's bed may have been the vessel that transported him on journeys of reflection and remembrance in the real world, room travel is something which has also featured in fiction. In Gavin Lambert's *The Slide Area*, about the lonely souls living along the Pacific Palisades in 1950s Los Angeles, in the chapter 'The End of the Line', about the eccentric Countess Marguerite Osterberg-Steblech, it seems as if the narrative was inspired directly from the writings of de Maistre and Karr. Lambert tells the story of the Countess, living in a big, grey house in the twisting hills of coastal California where "Stateliness hangs in the air" (Lambert, 1954, p.55) but with the impression that most of the mansion's rooms above the city are filled with "furniture draped with old sheets and blinds pulled down" (ibid., p.55). Marguerite has just turned 79 and her health is failing. She is blind, mostly deaf and cared for by her nieces Pia and Carlotta. While the Countess's fortune remains intact despite its journey across war ravaged Europe, her nieces are worried that she will fritter away the last of her money—which they are due to inherit—before her death, as her eccentricities expand. A prime example of the niece's worry being the $90,000 tiara the Countess leaves on the table of a gala dinner as a donation. Before she is rendered immobile for good, Marguerite requests her nieces take her on one last overseas adventure to revisit her favourite European destinations.

After the Countess has not been heard from for months, a friend, Mark, visits the house to investigate her disappearance. Initially the mansion seems deserted, though as he listens closely Mark can hear bursts of flamenco in the distance. As he moves to the window outside the living room, he discovers that the space has been cleared and a make-shift railway carriage has been constructed in the centre, with a luggage rack, sliding glass doors on one side and a mechanical device under the seat of Marguerite's chair, allowing it to rock gently from side-to-side. With this discovery Mark watches the Countess's room travel in full swing: "With ungainly flamenco movements, Pia circled the carriage. She clicked a pair of castanets, stretched her long neck and flapped her arms like a hungry distracted bird. From the couch Carlotta clapped her hands and shouted an occasional 'Olé!'" (Lambert, 1954, p.71). Three record players stood in the room imitating flamenco music, train sounds and the ambience of Madrid in July. The nieces had decided to allow their aunt to travel to Europe, though to preserve their inherited fortune, she would not leave the house. They ordered guidebooks, wind machines, electric fires for heat and fans to simulate cold. What followed was a room journey through Europe for Countess Marguerite. "She had attended Mass at Notre-Dame, the living-room sprayed with incense and Pia tinkling a bell in her ear" (ibid., p.76). They had taken her gambling in Monte Carlo, to the banks of the Danube to listen to old waltzes and to the canals of Venice aboard a rowing boat tethered to the edge of her swimming pool.

When questioned of their fraud they are absolute, "Would it make her more happy to really be in Venice?" (Lambert, 1954, p.79) asks Pia, both nieces contending that it might be a fatal expedition due to her failing health. This is not to say that the room travel made everything easy on Pia and Carlotta. "Cooking is the worst" (ibid., p.79) they lament as they must learn new dishes from every visited country daily. It seems that Countess Marguerite has the last laugh, though, as she demands to travel somewhere new and the nieces transport her to Marrakech, where she drinks mint tea and listens to the flutes and drums of the Moroccan marketplace for six months while reclined on cushions and sheep skin rugs. Pia and Carlotta conjure storms, move heaters into the room for summer and even invent a terrorist coup with broken windows and recorded machine gun fire, yet they still cannot get her to leave until finally a gala dinner with her peers draws her back 'home' after many months abroad.

Just as Mark's view of this close travel is initially sceptical, he eventually appreciates the imagination and ingenuity of the nieces' approach for what it is. This travelling imagination is another aspect that will linger post-pandemic—where we re-think the need to go to Bali and where the prospect of setting up a bus made of dining chairs and blankets on a rainy Saturday with our children can bring as much joy as the snippets of experience in a $10,000 mini-break.

Contemporary close travel

While much of the initial experimentations and examples of close travel concentrate on those periods bracketing the Romantic era from the 17th century onwards, surprisingly this has not been a style or sub-genre which has diminished in this modern era of increased technology and shorter attention spans. While many guidebooks have become largely superfluous due in large part because of technology and the prevalence of travellers using portable devices such as phones and tablets to gain instant reviews and directions rather than relying on cumbersome and out-dated guides, the focus on new and more considered forms of travel narratives has brought about a fresh interest in the more thoughtful, ethical and engaged traveller and travel writing.

De Maistre's motivation, in part, was to present travel as something attainable for those who were sick, destitute, timid or lazy. As a counterpoint, with so much choice for the traveller in the 21st-century pre-COVID world, from package tours to Antarctica to dark-tourism experiences in Cambodia, this has prompted some modern travel writers to pause their wanderlust and re-focus their gaze on the things around them as de Maistre did.

A Week at the Airport

In his book *A Week at the Airport: A Heathrow Diary* (2009), Alain de Botton inhabits London Heathrow's Terminal 5 as a writer in residence. He does so to try to understand the airport as a destination in itself and as a location with a distinct culture and 'home' to many intriguing people. "I arrived at the airport on a train from central London early on a Sunday evening, a small roller case in hand and no further destination for the week" (de Botton, 2009, p.16).

De Botton sets up a desk in the departure hall to pen his close travel narrative, confined, just like de Maistre, in his chosen enclosure for the duration of his stay. And so he reflects on people's body language and the 'politeness' of forced encounters at the airport; the first during a room service delivery in his airport hotel room:

> It is a strange moment when two adult men meet each other, one naked save for a complimentary dressing gown, the other (newly arrived in England from the small Estonian town of Rakvere and sharing a room with four others in nearby Hillingdon).
>
> *(De Botton, 2009, p.20)*

De Botton investigates the journey of the onboard meals for all flights at the airport, the backstories of the luggage carried by passengers through departures—from flat screen TVs for relatives in Accra, to six dark green suitcases full of souvenirs bound for Kashmir. De Botton reflects on the hope and anger he witnesses as people go about their business—leaving for holidays, returning from business trips, boarding flights to meet family or working shifts in British Airway's check-in counter, all together for a few brief moments before departing again—with his immersed and stationary presence there to witness it all.

This gives his experience and the more significant thoughts as to why we travel and how we treat one another during these encounters much more time than a traditional 'horizontal' voyage would permit. De Botton comes to understand that the loudspeaker announcements every few minutes come from two women, either Juliet or Margaret, that Ana-Marie from Transylvania is the cleaner assigned to his section and that after chatting to the head of British Airways as they wander through the terminal, he decides that in another life he and Willie Walsh could have become friends because of their unusual travel encounter.

De Botton clearly relishes the experience, though it does instil a sense of fear in the writer, that this new focus will lead him further into the notion of close experiences and domestic adventure: "I worried that I might never have another reason to leave the house" (de Botton, 2009, p.106). This rethinking of the focus of travel writing as demonstrated by de Botton, revisits Forsdick's idea of the concentric circles of attention possible with vertical travel. There is an '(in)exhausibility' (Forsdick, 2019) to this travel approach as it presents more layers, perspectives and ideas around place, the deeper the writer immerses within the experience.

Despite this excitement over the potential of close travel, de Botton comes to an interesting conclusion: that the notion of travel is always loaded in the modern era with our rationale for travelling in the first place—that travel becomes a space for time out, recharge, reconnection, exploration, generosity, and emotion as much as it does a voyage to a new destination:

> Travel agents would be wiser to ask us what we hope to change about our lives rather than simply where we wish to go. The notion of the journey as a harbinger of resolution was once an essential element of the religious pilgrimage, defined as an excursion through the outer world undertaken in an effort to promote and reinforce an inner evolution.
>
> *(De Botton, 2009, p.104)*

There is something familiar about de Botton's identification of vertical travel here. Pre-COVID the airport of our home cities would often be very familiar, yet completely foreign in the same moment. We'd know where the good coffee was and the cleanest toilets, yet what about the stories of the people who worked there, and the stories exploring how everything works behind the scenes? Many of us have had a closer appreciation of this type of travel without realising it in the past as we've slept in airports across the world waiting for early morning connections, glimpsing some of the layers that exist in these purgatorial places.

My own experience of this came a few years ago in Madrid. While researching another project at the airport—my book *After Dark: A Nocturnal Exploration of Madrid*—I noticed that once I stopped and slowed down, it was possible to see these layers that existed in Madrid's Barajas Terminal 4. In the wake of the 2008 financial crisis the levels of homelessness and unemployment in the city were significant—reflecting the 6 million unemployed across Spain at its peak. As I sat on a bench at Barajas Airport I noticed that travellers had a speed and posture to them—travellers' eyes are far off, either thinking of home and where they need to be, or purposely striding from counter to gate to corridor with mechanical purpose. In between this movement I began to notice those camouflaged people moving with a different gait across the shining white floors and underneath the domed ceilings. A man pushed a trolley laden with Ikea bags and rattled the drinks left behind by departed travellers. Another wore a suit jacket, yet his lack of socks and empty laptop bag suggested another purpose. One resident rolled out his sleeping bag, folded his clothes and positioned his shoes behind the Iberia counter as if it was an invisible bedroom. As I looked closer, I spoke to some of the 40 residents of Barajas who would commute into the airport each evening for the bathrooms, hot water, and safe spaces. Sefa, a Bulgarian immigrant, told me of his past as an electrician in the city, Geraldo a former police officer now concerned with the 'resident's' safety and protected the citizens for donations of cigarettes, and Rafael, a Venezuelan academic spent his days at free museums and galleries in Madrid before travelling out to the airport with his wife each night, never going anywhere beyond Terminal 4 in their own form of vertical travel.

'Another life in Paris'

Another example of modern close travel comes from Meg Watson in her article 'Another life in Paris' for the Australian *The Saturday Paper* which focuses on her experience inhabiting another person's space as an Airbnb guest in Paris. "On my first night in Canelle's bed, I watch *Midnight in Paris* and drink rosé from one of her stained teacups" (Watson, 2014).

The presence of Airbnb has undoubtedly changed the way many people travel (pre-COVID). But, as displayed in Watson's writing, it also affords travel writers the opportunity to utilise this closeness and sense of focus in a novel manner by embracing the changes in the way people travel and write about it. "I can't help but think of it as someone living a version of my own life with different faces around them, different words to express the same emotions" (Watson, 2014).

Within the intimacy of the apartment Watson shows the reader a closer and more nuanced perspective of Paris. The voyeurism of this close approach also allows the reader to appreciate the sameness of a travel experiences once they concentrate on more mundane encounters:

> Travel is really equal parts curiosity and delusion. By buying a plane ticket and taking leave from work, in some small way we step out of ourselves. We try the local cuisine and create new shapes with our tongues to form words we've never heard before. We roam strange city streets and try to tessellate ourselves into crowds. As Marcel Proust said, 'The real voyage of discovery consists not in seeking new landscapes, but in having new eyes.'
>
> *(Watson, 2014)*

From a contemporary perspective Watson's close writing embraces the affordances of the 21st century by utilising a technological and touristic advancement such as Airbnb in order to obtain this new, closer perspective. While it does give the author a more nuanced and personal experience (in Paris, in this example), Watson writes of the conflicted ideas around authenticity this perspective also raises. She writes about the ethics of both Airbnb, as it creates imbalances in the tourist economy of cities such as Paris and Barcelona where locals rent out family homes and offer sub-par accommodation to meet the growing tourist demand to 'live like a local'. Watson believes initially that the heavy brass key in her pocket grants her access to the secret inner life of the city, yet at the same time she notes the contradictions to this idea—there is an identical Ikea blanket on her bed back in Australia and her time in Canelle's apartment is bookended by the prompt to fill in a visitor's book for the next Airbnb guests to read—loosening this notion of the unique and authentic nature of the experience.

Isolarion: A Different Oxford Journey

In his book *Isolarion*, James Attlee extends the notion of close travel, or a "home tour" as Kinsley (2019, p.119) calls it, further when he decides that he needs a break from the everyday monotony of his life, and a pilgrimage he could not ignore presents itself to him. Attlee's issue is that because of work, family, and general life commitments he no longer has the means or the desire to pack a bag, book a ticket to a far-off location and toil for months on end away from his familiar life as his travels once compelled him to do. As such, he arrives at a compromise: "Gradually it dawned on me that the voyage I needed to make began in my own neighbourhood, within a few minutes' walk of my front door" (Attlee, 2007, p.xiv) And so he goes exploring his local environment in suburban Oxford, a city mostly known for its past and the prestige of its university. "This city has dispatched anthropologists, explorers, scientists, authors, and poets to every nation represented on Cowley Road" (ibid., p.xvi). He commits to flip his gaze and see Cowley Road through their eyes. Attlee realises from his long history of travel abroad that there is an opportunity to rethink how he travels and what he learns from the experience, "I have to learn to travel more thoughtfully, to slip beneath the surface and explore more deeply. Space is relative. One aim of my pilgrimage will be to connect me to the neighbourhood in which I live" (ibid., p.x).

He walks past Asian grocery stores, transfixed by the stories revealed from the litter on the pavement—boxes of Spanish oranges, radishes from Lazio, and Indian fruit boxes. He revels in the answers to questions he poses—about the origin of fresh sugarcane stalks at the counter, yellow dates offered during Ramadan and the stories of *patra* leaves used by the Cambodian and Gujarati communities instead of plates for eating their meals. As further examples of close travel encounters along Cowley Road, Attlee visits immersion tank facilities, jewellers, tailors, restaurants, former leper institutions, and churches—places he'd never stopped to examine closely before, though these are all on this one stretch of road and now part of his vertical travel experience.

This type of close travel, though, peeling back layers of the familiar, is not without its ethical challenges. Attlee discovers that as he seeks to understand Cowley Road, it does not afford him the usual anonymity that many travel encounters allow. Attlee writes about his attempts to enter the notorious blue door of Cowley Road's adult sex store, which is adjacent to a local bus stop, "Whenever I pass and think about entering, the queue waiting for a bus appears inordinately long and made up almost exclusively of people known to me" (Attlee, 2007, p.67).

What makes Attlee's journey a valuable contribution to vertical travel writing is its imaginative use of psychogeography, by demonstrating a novel way of "apprehending our urban environment", as Coverly (2006, p.13) writes. Attlee focuses on encounters "that atomise and defamiliarise everyday spaces, and encourage attention to their unexpectedly fractal details", according to Forsdick's definition (Forsdick, 2019, p.101), where he revisits locations he's walked past for years, and uses this new technique to look closer at people and places he has not considered previously. Attlee is challenging his own notion of travel and the popular assumption of what is worth visiting in Oxford as an outsider. He draws these experiences out in slow, methodical detail to demonstrate the verticality possible in somewhere so familiar to him.

Another interesting inclusion in the vertical travel cannon is space travel. Where else is there such an apt comparison for the idea of close travel, of paying attention to one's surroundings as de Maistre did and drawing out, creatively and sensorily, deeper meaning in a 'travel' experience, than that of an astronaut, thousands of kilometres above earth, looking down on it while trapped in a metal box hurtling through space?

In Scott Kelly's *Endurance* he tells the story of his life as an astronaut, in particular he details the physical and psychological experience of living for a year confined inside the ISS (International Space Station). In an interesting segue to the next chapter of this book, this is possibly the only example of vertical travel where the writer did not have any choice (except for the legal imperative of de Maistre to stay in his room), once he had departed Houston for the Kazakhstan desert launch site he was locked into his experience for a year.

Kelly tells the story of his time as a space traveller in diary-like format, though it is the attention to the little details, things that people who aren't astronauts or tech billionaires, that are the most intriguing for their sense of difference. On his final morning on earth, he wakes at 7am and has fried eggs and sausage. Despite humans landing on the moon in 1969, any form of space travel will remain a mystery to all but a select few. There are many examples of how unique this is as a 21st century offering of de Maistre's 'room travel'; he describes the only compartment on the ISS that is just for him, his sleeping pod—it is about the size of a phone booth, he vividly recalls the metallic smell of space as they dock into the ISS, the lack of silence with the constant hum of electronics and whirr of the cooling fans and the fact that the space station "doesn't feel like an object. It feels like a place" (Kelly, 2017, p.102) with its own personality. He has a computer built into the wall where he writes his dream journal each morning to observe what impact his situation has on the surreal nature of his dreams. Kelly's narrative makes space 'living' seem sweaty and hard work, with constant checks, adjustments and calibrations, even making sure that all tools and utensils are fastened with Velcro or duct tape so they don't float haphazardly through the zero gravity space. There are brief moments though where his observations show the earth from above, of the turquoise Bahamas to the smog covering Asia. Kelly writes that as they spin through space the lack of nature becomes depressing, so much so that one of his colleagues plays recordings of mosquitos so he feels more connected to the Earth. Kelly's writing on the toilet is particularly unique as an example of close travel writing, writing that one of the most essential elements of this form of travel "is a working toilet, and ours does more than just store waste—our urine processor distils our urine into drinking water" (ibid., p.188).

* * *

While the notion of close travel writing began with the room scale introspection of Xavier de Maistre in the 18th century, surprisingly it has not diminished as technology, style and altered reading habits influence the way travel literature is both read and produced. As a foil to the adaptations of modern travel life, close travel writing, with its renewed focus on the near at hand and the layers of our familiar surroundings, has increased the validity and creativity of the travel writing genre while also adding a deeper ethical component to travel. As I write this, and possibly many of you read this from your own homes during the ripples from COVID-19, the notion of rethinking is as valid as it has ever been in many of our lifetimes.

As Pettinger says: "To describe 'dwelling' as 'travel' is to transform it into something worth writing about" (Pettinger, 2019, p.277). This chapter has illuminated historical and contemporary examples where the notion of 'dwelling' as a travel writing technique allows for more nuanced and thoughtful perspectives. Forsdick expanded this idea further by suggesting that some travel writing involves the intersections of the horizontal journey and the vertical sense of depth, "reflecting the experimental potential of travel writing to propose new and often defamiliarising ways of viewing and engaging with elsewhere" (Forsdick, 2019, p.110).

While the initial prompt of not moving, not seeking adventure or physical challenge by staying close to home may run counter to what travel and travel writing has traditionally been seen as, it is this challenge—to acknowledge and explore a different way of thinking about the world which can ultimately expand our boundaries and its lasting impact post-COVID. According to Vuillemin who wrote in 1894, every person, "who has circled the globe twice has probably discovered less than the poor hermit who has taken a journey through his room" (cited in Stiegler, 2013, p.27).

References

Attlee, J (2007). *Isolarion: A Different Oxford Journey*. University of Chicago Press.

Burton, R (1860). *Lake Regions of Central Africa*. Longman & Roberts.

Carruthers, F (2020). 'Golden age' beckons for $23b caravan industry. *Australian Financial Review*, 16 August. Retrieved from www.afr.com/companies/tourism/golden-age-beckons-for-23b-caravan-industry-20200816-p55m5g. Accessed 20/9/21.

Coverley, M (2006). *Psychogeography*. Pocket Essentials.

Creech, B. (2014). The spectacle of past violence: travel journalism and dark tourism. In F Hanusch & E Fürsich (eds), *Travel Journalism: Exploring Production, Impact and Culture*. Palgrave Macmillan, pp. 249–266.

Cronin, M (2000). *Across the Lines: Travel, Language, Translation*. Cork University Press.

de Botton, A (2009). *A Week at the Airport: A Heathrow Diary*. Vintage.

de Maistre, X (2017 [1794]). *A Journey round My Room (and a Nocturnal Expedition round My Room)* (trans. H Attwell). Hurd and Haughton.

Forsdick, C (2019). Vertical travel. In A Pettinger & T Youngs (eds), *The Routledge Research Companion to Travel Writing*, pp. 99–112. Routledge.

Hagglund, B (2000). Tourists and travellers: Women's non-fictional writing about Scotland 1770–1830. Dissertation, University of Birmingham.

Hagglund, B (2010). Gendering the Scottish guidebook: Sarah Murray's companion and useful guide. *Women's Writing*, 17(1), 129–146.

Hagglund, B (2019). Domestic ritual. In C Forsdick, Z Kinsley, & K Walchester (eds), *Keywords for Travel Writing Studies: A Critical Glossary* (pp. 75–77). Anthem Press.

Karr, A (1845). *A Tour around My Garden*. (trans. JG Wood). Routledge.

Kelly, S (2017). *Endurance: A Year in Space, a Lifetime of Discovery*. Random House.

Kinsley, Z (2006). Travel and material culture: Commodity, currency, and destabilised meaning in women's home tour writing, *Studies in Travel Writing*, 10:2, 101–122.

Kinsley, Z (2019). Home tour. In C Forsdick, Z Kinsley, & K Walchester (eds), *Keywords for Travel Writing Studies: A Critical Glossary*. Anthem Press, pp. 119–121.

Lambert, G (1954). *The Slide Area*. Viking Press.

Lee, G (1974). Where our caravans have rested. *Country Life*.

Lee, J (2012). Alternative urban journeys: Italian travel writing and the Contromano series. *Studies in Travel Writing*, 16(2), 203–214.

Leiris, M (1984). *Raymond Roussel, In Havanna: Ein Romanfragment*. Syndikat.

Martin, A (2008). *Moving Scenes: The Aesthetics of German Travel Writing on England, 1783–*. Routledge.

Murray, S (1982 [1799]). *A Companion and Useful Guide to The Beauties of Scotland* (ed. WF Laughlan). Byway Books.

Onyx, J, & Leonard, R (2007). "The grey nomad phenomenon: Changing the script of aging". *International Journal of Aging & Human Development*, 64(4), 381–398.

Pettinger, A (2019). Vertical travel. In C Forsdick, Z Kinsley, & K Walchester (eds), *Keywords for Travel Writing Studies: A Critical Glossary*. Anthem Press, pp. 277–279.

Pratt, M (2002). *Imperial Eyes: Travel Writing and Transculturation*. Routledge.

Sharpley, R, & Stone, P (2009). *Darker Side of Travel: The Theory and Practice of Dark Tourism*. Channel View Publications.

Simons, M (2020). Winter's bounty. *The Saturday Paper*, 20–26 June. Retrieved from www.thesaturdaypaper.com.au/life/gardening/2020/06/20/winters-bounty/159257520010006#hrd (accessed 25 August 2020).

Stern, K (1805). *Auch eine Reiseauf meinem zimmer* (trans. B Stiegler). Leipzig.

Stiegler, B (2013). *Traveling in Place: A History of Armchair Travel* (trans. P Filkins). University of Chicago Press.

Stubbs, B (2019). *The Crow Eaters: A Journey Through South Australia*. New South Books.

Thompson, C (2011). *Travel Writing: The New Critical Idiom*. Routledge.

Twain, M (2010 [1869]). *The Innocents Abroad*. Wordsworth Editions.

Watson, M (2014). Another life in Paris, thanks to Airbnb. *The Saturday Paper*, 4–10 October. Retrieved from www.thesaturdaypaper.com.au/2014/10/03/another-life-paris-thanks-airbnb/14122957881047 (accessed 1 October 2020).

Youngs, T (2013). *The Cambridge Introduction to Travel Writing*. Cambridge University Press.

Youngs, T and Pettinger, A (2019). Vertical travel. In A Pettinger & T Youngs (eds), *The Routledge Research Companion to Travel Writing*. Routledge, pp. 99–112.

3

ILLNESS

While the prospect of touring your garden and delving deeply into the wonders of each plant can be charming, it involves a sense of choice; but what if you had no option but to remain in your room, to linger in your bed or, worse still, to be stuck inside your head, locked in and unable to leave?

Confinement becomes something different and altogether more harrowing when we look at it through the lens of illness. As such, the examples of creativity spawning from these locked in experiences can give us much to think about during the current pandemic and how it has allowed writers to travel beyond their circumstances. In the COVID-19 era we are aware of the impacts of the virus and the isolation it has imposed on all of us. During this period, though, it is also worth looking at the historical and cultural relationships between confinement and creativity and the potential to contextualise the current predicament, and to offer ideas, warnings or even optimism for the uncertainty ahead.

The COVID-19 pandemic has demonstrated how important creative pursuits are for all of us, whether that be as writers seeking to understand their isolation, or like many of us, to escape into a binge watched TV series, a YouTube album launch or into a book that helps us get through Zoom meetings, home school timetables and the ambiguity of our circumstances until the next day. The importance of creativity in times of isolation cannot be underestimated and the hope is that the present book offers the chance to understand our current conditions with greater context while also capturing a wider sense of what writing during times of isolation has created for the world.

As writer and English professor at the University of Richmond, Elisabeth Outka notes that the influence of a pandemic is, "a paradigm-shifting event that divides lives and cultures into a before and after. We will emerge changed, though how those changes will manifest is far from certain" (Outka, 2020). I have been writing this book during 2020 and 2021 and it often seems as if we are still in the eye of the

DOI: 10.4324/9781003243267-3

storm, in a centre that seems to continually change its circumference—close enough to still dream of the normal elements of life as they were before and to get frustrated when we can't obtain them, yet we're not far enough through to be able to reflect entirely on the virus's impact and how it might change us from a distance.

Just as Xavier de Maistre was confined to his room for the duration of his sentence yet he still managed to travel beyond his isolation in order to create his own literary identity from within confinement, there are many fascinating examples of writers and those who wrote of their experiences being restricted to their rooms, their beds and, in extreme cases, locked inside their own minds as forms of 'illness narrative'.

Contemporary writing

For Elisabeth Tova Bailey in her 2010 book *The Sound of a Wild Snail Eating*, this experience centred on the importance of the formation of a relationship, no matter how insignificant it might seem to outside eyes. Bailey was a healthy and active 34-year-old living on a farm in the northeastern United States. When she took a short holiday to Europe to the Alps to walk along cobbled lanes in small villages and above glacial lakes, she began to feel slightly off. Vivid dreams pre-empted her descent into sickness. She fainted and endured 10 days of fever before she was admitted to hospital on her return home. As the symptoms worsened still, she felt her body separating from her mind, her consciousness spiralling into a deep and distant abyss. Bailey was diagnosed with a mysterious bacterial pathogen rendering her largely immobile with severe neurological symptoms. She was moved to a white-walled bedsit to recuperate, and among the many personal items transported to her new quarters was the gift of a pot plant from a friend, filled with field violets and a small, solitary snail trailing along for the ride concealed in the foliage.

This time in isolation gave Bailey the time to reflect on her life and the significance of the things she took for granted, "Given the ease with which health infuses life with meaning and purpose, it is shocking how swiftly illness steals away those certainties" (Bailey, 2010, p.6).

Bailey lay in her bed, watching the movement of light on her walls. The days bled into weeks, and her writing and the perspective she portrayed slowly became calmer. She was perplexed by her friends, who could do whatever they liked and travel whenever they pleased, yet they are overwhelmed by the stresses of their everyday lives.

Yet with this stillness and slow passing of time she noticed the world of the snail on the table next to her bed in closer detail as she practiced life writing. First the snail seemed dead during the day as the empty shell did not move, though in the afternoons she began to see it emerge and slide across the sides of the pot plant and down to a discarded envelope. Each morning she woke to see the snail had eaten a small square portion of the paper, so she began to leave it food—dead petals from the violets initially—and she watched, confined to her bed, in the way that

Alphonse Karr might have observed his garden, while over the course of an hour the snail ate every morsel of the petal.

Bailey's world was so still and quiet that she could hear its tiny teeth gnawing on the foliage. All of a sudden this empty existence of hers had great meaning—she found a companion in the most unlikely place and this pushed her inside a world of wonder by concentrating more intently on the near-at-hand, "Survival often depends on a specific focus: a relationship, a belief or a hope balanced on the edge of possibility" (Bailey, 2010, p.15). Bailey realised that both she and the snail are living in landscapes not of their choosing and, while there is a sense of loss and longing, strangely it prompts them both to explore their new worlds in greater detail, as Bailey realised, she was not alone. The snail glided across vitamin bottles and drawings, all the while Bailey reflected on the objects in her room, remembering the doctor's box below her bed that was her grandfathers in the 1920s and the empathy he showed for those in his care—from men mauled by tigers in Burma to distraught farmers whose elephants needed their boils lanced.

As readers, possibly also reading this in our own isolation, it becomes apparent that the process of opening up to the snail, or looking closer and appreciating the intricacies of companionship, no matter how small, propel Bailey to express this creatively. On the surface of things, the book is about a woman in bed looking at a snail eating dead flowers, though when we look closer as well there is poetry and excitement in the language and we want to know what happens next, both to the writer and the snail as she arranges for a terrarium to be built next to her bed and their co-habitation extends. Bailey writes that finding the snail saved her, "the snail kept my spirit from evaporating" (Bailey, 2010, p.132). I would take this a step further, though, and claim that it was the writing and the attention of 'close travelling' in the encounter with the snail that played just as big a part—recalling the details of the snail's teeth, writing of the 118 tiny eggs hatching under the carefully placed ferns and mussel shells, contextualising its appreciation of space with her own and attaching a narrative with a beginning, middle and an end to her time with the snail in order to make sense of their whole shared encounter.

There are other creative examples that show the importance and insistence of stories when people are isolated through illness. The story of Jean-Dominique Bauby became world-renowned in the 1990s when the news of his illness, and the writing of his memoir *The Diving Bell and the Butterfly: A Memoir of Life in Death* (1998) spread through the world. Bauby was the editor-in-chief of French *Elle* magazine and while driving his nine-year-old son to the theatre he suffered a cerebrovascular seizure, a catastrophic stroke that rendered him immobile and locked inside his body, with the blinking of one eye his only way to communicate with the outside world.

Slowly, Bauby learned how to communicate, developing a special alphabet with the occupational therapists which they would read aloud, and he would blink to confirm each letter of his sentences, unlocking his thoughts to the world once again. With the help of a publisher's emissary he dictated, through 200,000 blinks, each letter of his memoir to explore his life post incident and to reflect on it pre-lock in. Bauby explained that his body felt as if it was trapped inside a solid diver's bell suit, submerged underwater, yet through the ability to tell his story he became free. "My cocoon becomes less oppressive, and my mind takes flight like a butterfly. There is so much to do. You can wander off in space or time, set out for Tierra del Fuego or for King Midas' court" (Bauby, 1998, p.13) he writes. With his newfound ability to be creative, his words are inspired. Interspersed between his daily medical rituals—remembering that aside from the slightest movements he is immobile, and he is delivering this book to us as if by telepathy through his carefully considered blinking—he writes of travel plans, a novel he intends to write and the recipe for a new fruit cocktail he wants to patent.

The writing from behind Bauby's closed door lets us in on the harsh and often tragic realities of his prognosis, of the alienation from others and the humiliation of wearing adult diapers, while also glimpsing the poetics he can now observe in the world that has closed in for him. His humour remains intact, "If I must drool, I may as well drool on cashmere" (Bauby, 1998, p.17) he writes of his refusal to wear a hospital gown. He writes of his ability to still travel imaginatively and the comfort the view of the lighthouse from the hospital terrace provides him, a guardian for those, like him, "castaways on the shores of loneliness" (ibid., p.29). In the end, just like Bailey and her snail, and Karr and his garden, there is a peacefulness that descends over Bauby from the bringing to life of his world. On the last page of his memoir, he writes of this feeling, "for the first time in a long while I don't have that awful sense of a countdown—the feeling triggered at the beginning of a holiday that inevitably spoils a good part of it" (ibid., p.130).

On 7 March 1997, ten days after the book was published, Jean-Dominique Bauby died of heart failure.

* * *

To take this exploration further as it relates to the sufferer's ability to travel inventively through or within their confinement, and while not necessarily defined as 'illness', the onset of vision or hearing impairment as examples of disability are interesting to consider for how writers have expressed themselves and found creativity from inside the restraints of these afflictions. As Brooks and Jackson write, "the disabled are very often, by necessity, stronger, more resilient, wiser and most certainly more inventive than a large proportion of the abled they live amongst" (Jackson & Brooks, 2016, p.7) and as a result there is a clear avenue for "autopathography" as Couser (1997) calls it, that being the autobiographical writing of illness and disability which is heightened due to the awareness "of one's mortality, threatening one's sense of identity, and disrupting the apparent plot of one's life" (ibid., p.5). This also then becomes a form of post-modern illness writing, where the personal and specific style of writing from within the illness is given preference over the unifying general view offered from those outside the affliction.

Narratives of hearing impairment, as Brueggemann writes, undo the assumptions around ability and agency and it often attests "to what deaf people, especially deaf people writing and reading, cannot do" (Brueggemann, 2000, p.316). Yet, as we have seen from Bauby and Bailey there is a richness of expression from within these afflictions which is often missed and that can alert us to the diverse sets of writing which have occurred around the broader themes of isolation and illness in the past. Couser writes "even though illness and disability represent forms of marginalization to which we are all vulnerable, they remain truly marginalized topics within the academy" (Couser, 1997, p.4) and even now within the pandemic, they remain under-served.

The importance of introspection when one is isolated through illness, and when the writer is psychologically able to facilitate their craft, demonstrates a fitting set of circumstances to write the stories of one's life. There is a broader significance here as well, that in the age of COVID, when the vast majority of the world are more tuned into their own prospects of unexpected illness and mortality, especially the middle-class citizens of comfortable Western countries in any case, it becomes something more noteworthy and narratable. "Perhaps, then, narratives of disability and illness serve to expose and dramatize what we would prefer to ignore most of the time, to arouse and (ideally) assuage our anxiety about our somatic selves", writes Couser (1997, p.9) to support this notion.

As I have written about previously, the notion of travel writing while blind is not new (Stubbs, 2016). It is interesting to consider though how vision impaired voyagers experienced travel in a conventional manner through some of their senses, while still relying on imagination and enthusiasm as part of their travel experience. The most notable blind traveller was Englishman James Holman in the 19th century, who lost his sight at 25 and subsequently travelled the world as an adventurer, "charting the Australian outback, escaping captivity in Siberia and hunting rogue elephants in Sri Lanka without ever 'seeing' any of it in a conventional sense" (ibid., p.129) while not letting his disability either define him or restrict his experiences. Furthermore, as Tilley writes, there was "a networked community of blind and visually impaired people using life writing for therapeutic, financial and political means in nineteenth-century Britain" (Tilley, 2017, p.98) to expand the horizons of both themselves as writers and the reading public.

This idea of looking, feeling, listening, or imagining a closer sense of travel to move beyond the affliction, echoes the experiences of de Maistre and the idea of a focus on the near-at-hand in order to appreciate the "skin of the light", as Hélène Cixous (1998, p.79) called it, and the extremities of the experience.

Hearing impairment and writing also offer an interesting interpretation of how writing can allow both physical and metaphorical movement through its practice. Despite the often-powerful cultural barriers to writing from within hearing impairment, where literacy in English or another language may be secondary to AUSLAN or sign language, Jessica White writes of Australian poet Judith Wright's relationship with deafness and how it enhanced her creative practice. The impairment reached into Wright's creative practice, directing her towards her vocation and influencing her style and themes. "Silence, for example, is prevalent in her oeuvre, as is her awareness of the limits of language. As someone who needed to strain constantly to hear, Wright also knew that meaning could easily break" (White, 2020, p.243).

This enhancement, and even direction of creative work as dictated by the sensation of being hearing impaired is also evident in the writing of renowned 19th century Australian writer and poet Henry Lawson, who became deaf at the age of 14—six years before he was first published. Tink writes that the experience of being hearing-impaired not only influenced Lawson's desire to write and to find creativity from within his disability, but it also strongly influenced his style, the themes he wrote about, the words he used and the rhythm of his prose. This gave his work a complexity and sense of precariousness that might not have always been discernible (Tink, 2016). She notes that on closer reading of his stories, the descriptions of place are vivid and transport the reader, though these scenes are often silent, except when Lawson offers a tactile sense of sound to allow the reader to experience the sense of place in the same manner he does, as in 'Brighten's Sister-in-Law':

> Those trees are always sigh-sigh-sighing—more of a sigh than a sough or the "whoosh" of gum-trees in the wind. You always hear them sighing, even when you can't feel any wind. It's the same with telegraph wires: put your head against a telegraph post on a dead, still day, and you'll hear and feel the far-away roar of the wires.
>
> *(Lawson, 2009, p.111)*

The details these writers with vision and hearing impairment could capture and how they could bring these elements vividly to life, to allow outsiders to appreciate not only the reality of the impairment and the impact of the coexistence with their conditions, but to also understand the disability's influence better on the style and tone of the narrative. This offers readers an appreciation of different creative approaches towards the 'limits' of an impairment. These writers also demonstrate how to utilise different perspectives and sensations, different ideas of what isolation can mean, and how notions of silence and stillness can inform and enrich narratives in unexpected ways.

Illness and fiction

While Daniel Defoe is better known for his novel *Robinson Crusoe* (more on that later), he was a journalist for most of his life and after living through the plague as a young boy, he collated his research—statistics, pamphlets, interviews and observations and combined them with fictional stories, into an early example of fictocriticism, "a cross between a novel, a *memento mori,* and a self-help book" (Defoe, 2003 [1722] p.xx), writes Cynthia Wall in the modern introduction to Defoe's book, to help give a voice to the untold stories of the plague in *A Journal of the Plague Year.* While the book has been analysed from scholars in diverse fields such as journalism, medicine and geography for its accuracy and Defoe's relationship with 'truth', reading this now, amidst our own pandemic, these quibbles and critiques become much less important as we look at the greater significance of his writing on plague, quarantine and confinement.

Defoe's writing of the *Journal* reflects a pattern we're all now somewhat familiar with. As Wall writes in the introduction of the narrator's digressions, his narrative is constantly "eddying and surging", the plot reflects the evolution of the plague itself as it retreats and attacks, escapes and is confined, re-enacting "his behaviour in his storytelling" (Defoe, 2003 [1722], p.xxx) and never quite allowing the reader to feel entirely comfortable.

Will Eaves wrote in the *Times Literary Supplement* in 2020 that Defoe's book "brims with recognizable situations" (Eaves, 2020) and it plays out the same tropes we see now of the rich escaping to country estates (or new countries for vaccination), while the poor are "condemned by the riskiest essential employments" (ibid.) and deemed powerless to contradict authority. Of Defoe's narrative structure, the main character is the epidemic, presented this way to allow us to immerse into the story and appreciate, as with our own pandemic, how it stains all readings, viewings and other creative pursuits, it doesn't reassure us that there will be a hero to deliver us from the plague and, as Eaves writes, just as with now, the underlying premise is "should I say or should I go?".

Defoe's book filled an important space when it was published, as he notes early on, with the book's narrator H.F., a saddler, stating that, "We had no such thing as printed News Papers in those Days, to spread Rumours and Reports of Things" (Defoe, 2003 [1722], p.3) to provide some sort of context or historical perspective, and even if the text blends the real with the invented, it captures the stories of those impacted by the plague. There is an eerie similarity reading this book during COVID-19. Defoe writes of the slow, but gradual spread of the disease across Europe, he includes a daily counter of the dead, he details of how the Government install "Turn-pikes and Barriers on the Road, to prevent Peoples travelling" (ibid., p.10) and whether he should flee London for a less plague infested (and locked down) location in the country and take his brother's advice that "the best Preparation for the Plague was to run away from it" (ibid., p.11).

Most impactfully when *A Journal of the Plague Year* is read while us readers in the 21st century are also in lockdown, it provides a glimmer of perspective. 300 years on and there are still the same stories of people unwilling to take the plague seriously, "addicted to Prophesies, and Astrological Conjurations, Dreams, and old Wives Tales" (Defoe, 2003 [1722], p.22), concerns for business and finance amidst the restrictions and panic, the same religious and spiritual searching for the deeper meaning of what was happening and what H.F. should do as a reaction to this, though there are also thousands of deaths each day and stories throughout where "whole Families were so entirely swept away" (ibid., p.221) in a matter of days and of the mass burial sites in London where "Womens Sculls were distinguish'd by their long hair" (ibid., p.223) to highlight how precarious things could be. Defoe writes of the decree that ordered each infected pest house be shut up and guarded by two watchmen 24 hours a day for a month until the sickness had passed, trapping all 'inmates' inside for the quarantine period, often condemning all inside to die along with the initial infected person. Each plague-ridden house would be daubed with a large red cross, doors would be locked from the outside and if anyone attempted to escape, they would be tracked down and carried back inside during the night and the "dismal Shrieks and Out-cries" (ibid., p.55) could be heard throughout the neighbourhood. Yet, despite this hopelessness, Defoe writes of the many families who would unscrew the door locks, sneak through the alleys of adjoining houses, bribe their guards or even blow up the watchmen with gun powder to live, and die, on their own terms.

* * *

Perhaps a more influential and foreboding example of writing and confinement as it relates to illness from the 20th century comes from French Algerian journalist and philosopher Albert Camus. His 1947 book *The Plague* is about the spread of mysterious illness passed first through rats, and then across the air to humans in a coastal Algerian town. As the citizens succumb to coughing fits, bulbous lymph nodes and unexplained bleeding they are faced with quarantine, uncertainty and disinfection squads as the disease progresses. *The Plague*, when engaged with during COVID-19, is often chilling for its premonitions and the demonstration of Camus's absurdist view of the world in which the book takes place.

As Camus writes, "There have been as many plagues in the world as there have been wars, yet plagues and wars always find people equally unprepared" (Camus, 1947, p.30). The calmness of Camus's writing from within the confinement of Oran's plague demonstrates his endorsement of absurdism, where the conflict of the inherent human need to find meaning in situations is juxtaposed against the inability for one to find purpose amidst this effort as the plague indiscriminately kills children, lovers and anyone in its random path.

Camus writes in his essay *The Myth of Sisyphus* of his philosophy:

> At this point of his effort man stands face to face with the irrational. He feels within him his longing for happiness and for reason. The absurd is born of this confrontation between the human need and the unreasonable silence of the world.
>
> *(Camus, 1991 [1955], p.28)*

Despite the seeming hopelessness of the Oranians' situation, and of their inability to control it, there is continual effort to circumvent this hopelessness—even writing letters is forbidden—as it may transmit the disease to the outside world, yet people constantly scheme ways for them to be smuggled out so as not to lose morale. "There were no longer any individual destinies, but a collective history that was the plague, and feelings shared by all" (Camus, 1947, p.129). In this exile at home, as the central character Dr Reiux discusses their predicament with Tarrou after they hear the local priest giving a sermon on the meaning he attributes to the plague, that it is obviously God's will and one that the people of Oran must submit to, Tarrou decides that the only meaning to be found in this situation is one of peace, "they're miserable because they don't let themselves go" (ibid., p.154) he decides as the only response to this uncertainty.

The Plague also highlights the humanist elements we see as it relates to our current 'plague'. It is interesting, this playing out of the humanist theory from Camus's most famous work—we see the selfishness of world leaders in 2021 similarly represented in the actions of the doctors of Oran as they 'decide' whether they are dealing with the plague or not, despite the streets of dead rats, the quarantine measures and the rising contagion indicating the obvious. Camus manipulates the narrative to push us to ponder the semantics of how those with a voice 'play' the scenarios out with thinly veiled and calculated optimism so that panic does not spread at the same rate as the disease. A shopkeeper hordes goods to sell them at inflated prices in the hope of finding financial purpose to this disease, yet he too succumbs to the disease and is discovered with "tins of food under his bed when they came to fetch him" (Camus, 1947, p.63), much like the toilet paper fiasco in Australia in 2020–2021.

There is something of the absurdism presented in *The Plague* also seen in Behrouz Boochani's *No Friend but the Mountains* as Boochani descends into the madness of his incarceration—unable to accept the uncertainty and monotony of his situation, while still able to conflate this experience into a narrative so that the outside reader may appreciate the meaning of his ordeal from a literary sense, while grappling with the nihilism and meaninglessness his situation is given by his captors.

One thing COVID-19 seems to have done is made all of us more acutely aware of the world we live in. We're now hyper-sensitive to our own illnesses, where a sore throat is something we might have previously ignored, it is now loaded with meaning and significance. Only a few months ago we might have been used to the regular Monday morning game with our children, when they complain that they're too sick for school, punctuating the request with a forced cough. Now we pivot at the first sniffle from our kids and look at co-workers blowing their noses in the office with secret contempt. Only a few months ago so many of us were too busy to pay close attention to our health and wellbeing, just like the visiting friends that Elisabeth Tova Bailey noticed from her quiet bedroom. Now as we spend weeks on end in our apartments and houses, we're so much more aware of the lumps, cavities, and bumps in our lives and what they might mean.

The time behind closed doors because of COVID-19 has also shone a much brighter light on our relationships. We are more tuned into the minutia of our friendships and the small cracks on the walls of our marriages and partnerships than we would have had time to address previously. The time in isolation has offered space to reconsider and better understand the precariousness of work, especially for those in the creative industries and humanities. The pandemic has not only exposed how hollow the PR descriptions of the 'nimble' and 'agile' places we work are, but it's also made many of us realise how much we all live in the little pig's straw house, when we all assumed we were the ones who lived in the brick house in the suburbs.

At the same time, during this isolation we might also remember those subtle, little things that keep us together—the shorthand we know about our partners' and friends' preferences and moods and the awareness of the vulnerability of all our lives in a way that has not happened for a generation. If, as Elisabeth Outka writes, there will be a before and after mentality to the world, I hope that this generates a new swathe of writing and creativity which captures this appreciation and awareness of the importance of the little things and how fleeting they might ultimately be.

If there is a positive from this it is that we are now more finely tuned into the world, and that we may not, even if for just a few years, take the lives we live for granted in quite the same way.

The pandemic of 1918

In this examination of illness and isolation there is an inevitable juxtaposition to be drawn with what is happening now and the influenza epidemic of 1918–1919 that killed up to 100 million people worldwide. While we live through the expansion of the COVID-19 virus, there are obvious comparisons with the pandemic which occurred across the world in the aftermath of the First World War. While the finer details are now resurfacing, many of the aspects of the 1918 influenza escaped from general knowledge for a long period despite the fact that nearly 1 in 3 people around the world became infected with this 'black flu' and 5 per cent of the world's population died as a result. As Outka writes in her evocatively titled essay '"Wood for the coffins ran out": Modernism and the shadowed afterlife of the influenza pandemic', "despite inflicting five to ten times more causalities than the First World War, the flu was, for a time at least, seemingly forgotten" (Outka, 2014, p.937).

In a now sobering premonition, Tegan Taylor wonders in a 2018 article whether, "in a modern world, with our knowledge of viruses and our advanced medicines, could something similar happen again?" (Taylor, 2018). She concludes that it is not just possible, but probable, and how the world fares compared to 1918 will largely depend on containment and cooperation.

The post war pandemic did not evolve from Spain yet seeing as the Spanish were neutral in the First World War and their government did not place the same restrictions on the post-war press, the spread and impacts of the virus were more widely reported and understood there as opposed to Germany and the UK, for example, which did not want to display weakness or a lack of morale in the immediate aftermath of the conflict. According to Taylor, the virus was most likely to have emerged from Kansas in the US and spread initially by returned soldiers—with 5500 UK soldiers dying in the first wave alone. The virus spread quickly as people travelled across the world in close quarters at the completion of the war. The three epicentres were the port cities of Freetown (Sierra Leone), Brest (France), and Boston (Massachusetts), and it tore through seemingly young and healthy populations with devastating symptoms, some sufferers bleeding from the eyes, ears and nose as it attacked and turned their skin a pallid grey from the lack of oxygen saturation and a mahogany colour in the moments before death as sufferers' lungs filled with fluid. Despite this, pandemics had occurred before, and in juxtaposition to the horrors of the war just passed, it was barely given coverage in the press. The *Times* reported that "the cause of the disease was the dry, windy Spanish spring … an unpleasant and unhealthy season at all times", even noting that its arrival to their shores was cheerfully anticipated (25 June 1918) such was the seriousness it was afforded.

The pandemic did not arrive in Australia until the third wave, with the ease of shutting the borders before air travel was common allowing the continent to escape the worst. Despite this, 12,000 people still died and one third of Sydney became infected.

The *Sydney Morning Herald* stated on 3 February 1919 that a "danger greater than war faces the State of New South Wales and threatens the lives of all":

> Everyone shall wear a mask. Those who are not doing so are not showing their independence—they are only showing their indifference for the lives of others—for the lives of the women and the helpless little children who cannot help themselves.
>
> *(Taylor, 2018)*

Even celebrated children's author May Gibbs was enlisted to create artworks which would prompt people to wear a mask.

Despite the rapid spread of the 1918 influenza across the world, this did not stifle the writing of the pandemic either; if anything it provided a visceral premise and an urgency in people to note down their stories. Writing during the 1918–1919 period showed how people were creatively and spiritually altered from the impact of the disease and the subsequent confinement occurring so soon after the war—leading to an increased output of religious work, and of all things, the emergence of zombie literature, as millions died across the world. The fact that many of these links with creativity and the pandemic have not resonated significantly until recent times says more about the era, as it occurred in the shadow of the First World War and the world was in a state of grief, unable to fully process the dual tragedies, especially, as Outka writes, the millions of deaths from the flu were seen as largely pointless and blameless when compared to the horrific scenes from the battlefields across Europe and the influenza's "shadowed position" (Outka, 2014, p.938).

The 1918 influenza impacted many writers and artists directly, Guillaume Apollinaire died from it; DH Lawrence, Katherine Anne Porter, and Edvard Munch barely survived their own infections, "even T. S. Eliot felt his brain was affected by his bout with the illness" (Outka, 2014, p.938).

Direct literary treatment of the pandemic as a central ordeal was rare in the UK and the US, in both literature and historical writing. Outka contending that the influenza's status as a shadow trauma was the most credible reason for this reaction.

TS Eliot wrote *The Waste Land* after having suffered the flu himself, all the while worried that it had somehow left lasting cerebral impact as he wrote his many-layered poem, turning "uncertainty into a climate, with its fogs, its corpse-haunted domestic landscape, its pervasive sense of living death, and its delirious language" (Outka, 2020).

Gripped by fever from the influenza, journalist Katherine Anne Porter was transported through the delirium into a paradise free of pain and suffering that offered her clarity. Porter survived and turned her experience into the modernist novella *Pale Horse, Pale Rider*, which was one of the few literary pieces written directly about the epidemic. Porter recounted that the experience, "simply divided my life … and after I was in some strange way altered … it took me a long time to go out and live in the world again" (Outka, 2020).

Porter's story echoes the duality of the world post-war, where, just like before and after an illness, it leaches into everything else going on around the characters. In *Pale Horse, Pale Rider* the main character, Miranda is delirious with the illness hallucinating that her partner, Adam is variously giving her medication, going to the shops for ice cream and cigarettes, or, when it seems the fever is at its worst, dying on a continual loop in her mind.

> "It's as bad as anything can be," said Adam, "all the theaters and nearly all the shops and restaurants are closed, and the streets have been full of funerals all day and ambulances all night—"
>
> *(Porter, 2012 [1939], p.300)*

As Miranda endures the sickness, confused and equally placing the reader in a state of confusion, we learn that as the world celebrates the end of the war, she receives mail that her Adam died while fighting in Europe, though her delusions mask the fact that he died from the flu in camp while waiting to head to the front. She recovers from the influenza, though the ripples of her dreams, and the dual impact of both the war and the pandemic linger:

> She lay on a narrow ledge over a pit that she knew to be bottomless, though she could not comprehend it; the ledge was her childhood dream of danger, and she strained back against a reassuring wall of granite at her shoulders, saying desperately, Look, don't be afraid, it is nothing, it is only eternity.
>
> *(Porter, 2012 [1939], p.324)*

The horror writer HP Lovecraft also utilised the 1918 influenza to create the sort of blood thirsty, dishevelled and wandering zombies intent on infecting the healthy that we've since seen with George Romero's *Night of The Living Dead* and in the TV series *The Walking Dead*. Lovecraft was surrounded by the dead and infected where he lived on Rhode Island and he utilised this atmosphere for his stories. In his modern take on *Frankenstein* with his story 'Herbert West: Reanimator' the main characters, West and Dan Cain, are doctors in a small town doing postgraduate work at Myskatonic University, prone to experiment with corpses in dimly lit basements when the pandemic strikes. "Through the fevered town had crept a curse which some said was greater than the plague, and which some whispered was the embodied daemon-soul of the plague itself", wrote Lovecraft (1985 [1922], p.26).

West 'reanimates' himself and prowls through the neighbourhood in darkness with Cain as his assistant looking for victims to experiment with—an embodiment of the monstrous damage the flu did through the same streets:

> The pale enthusiast now applied some last perfunctory tests for absolute lifelessness, withdrew satisfied, and finally injected into the left arm an accurately measured amount of the vital elixir, prepared during the afternoon with a greater care than we had used since college days, when our feats were new and groping.
>
> *(Lovecraft, 1985 [1922], p.40)*

Lovecraft's subsequent zombie stories also reflected much of the xenophobic panic that has occurred during COVID-19, Lovecraft amplifying the terror of invading foreign hordes and inherent racism directed at those seen as responsible. One enduring element Lovecraft highlighted with his influenza zombies, though, was that they were far worse than anything brought up by the war or the pandemic, despite the fact that these monsters could be seen and defeated.

Who or what will we ultimately blame, both from a literary and an existential sense when we don't have the remnants of a world war to react against? Of course there has been racism and xenophobia as the first impulses of many people and publications, though as this experience elongates will there be a rash of conventional Good vs Evil novels released to reassure us of the hero's journey of our lives, or will it be more subtle, like the sound of a snail or the appreciation of the afternoon sun after a week of gloom in the way we tell stories about this period we've all shared?

Outka contends that there is a lot to learn from the previous pandemic and much we can pay attention to from an artistic and cultural sense:

> The literature that arose from the influenza pandemic speaks to our current moment in profound ways, offering connections in precisely the realms where art excels: in emotional landscapes, in the ways a past moment reverberates into the present, in the ineffable conversation between the body's experiences and our perception of the world.
>
> *(Outka, 2020)*

* * *

As Tegan Taylor wrote in her ABC article, understanding the past is important for how we deal with the pandemics of the future. Now that it is upon us, beyond the medical perspective this awareness can also provide us with context to see how,

FIGURE 3.1. Charles Nuttall's cartoons of the influenza for *The Bulletin*
Source: courtesy of the National Archives of Australia. NAA: CP567/1, BOX 4

creatively speaking, the 1918 pandemic was articulated and understood from a local viewpoint as well. In Australia there was a notable literary and creative impact from those who found inspiration, or the compulsion to express themselves during the virus despite, or perhaps because of the pandemic.

Notable cartoonist Charles Nuttall, who worked for the Melbourne *Punch* and the Sydney *Bulletin*, drew the illustration shown in Figure 3.1 to further prompt creative attention on the pandemic. It followed with the caption: "Melbourne, February, 1919. No Sir—These are not Anarchists en route to a rendezvous. They are really nice people, going to attend a Sabbath evening Church service."

Political cartoonist and war artist Will Dyson, who practised his craft with a young Norman Lindsay on the streets of Melbourne, and drew some of the most cutting wartime comics of the era, lost his wife to the pandemic and wrote a collection of poetry in her honour called *Poems: In Memory of a Wife Who Died*, which reads as 38 pages of grief expressed through his words:

> There is no soft beatitude in Death:
> Death is but death;
> Nor can I find
> Him pale and kind
> Who set that endless silence on her
> Death is but death.
>
> *(Dyson, 1919)*

Perhaps surprisingly, there was still space for satire as the third wave of the influenza arrived in Australia, with *The Bulletin* publishing an article on the unfortunate reworking required for a production of *Romeo and Juliet*:

> An elaborate Shakespearean season promised to New York theatre goers has been postponed because the expected Juliet was detained in quarantine.
>
> Poor Romeo in loneliness
> Must sigh the long night through,
> With nought to love, nought to caress,
> And nothing much to do.
>
> *(Turner, 1919)*

When the virus finally made it to South Australia on 8 February 1919 the states closed their borders and the Jubilee Exhibition Building was turned into an isolation hospital.

As Marie Larsen wrote, "Due to the closing of the state borders, many holidaying South Australians found themselves stranded in Victoria" (Larsen, 2019). On 26 February 1919, after much ambiguity and uncertainty, arrangements were finally put in place for non-infected South Australians to be transported via train from Melbourne to South Australia.

Despite the dire circumstances, people separated themselves into 100 military tents along with stretchers, mattresses, lighting, and a water supply. Even though much of the outside opinion was negative regarding the infected detainees, they made the best of it and called their experience a 'big picnic'. There was an entertainment committee and a daily evening concert, including a poetry prize at the conclusion of their isolation. The group even released a booklet of creative outputs, essays, stories, and poems from their experience, titled: *Normal: Souvenir of the Quarantine Camp, Jubilee Oval, Adelaide, Feb. 26th–Mar. 5th, 1919* (Normal, 1919). They named the booklet as such because the virus influenced so many people from all walks of life. They had not done anything wrong; they were simply 'normal' people making the best of it during the "Great Epidemic" as they called it in the camp.

There are many highlights in the booklet, with poems, letters, a daily newspaper, and a selection of quarantine limericks. Here one young boy details his experience:

> Influenza is a disease what [sic] you catch in Sydney and Melbourne, it's a germ that moves on four legs, and keeps us away from school, my mother says she wishes it would last for ever as we don't have things to do and only have one bath a day.
>
> *(Normal, 1919, p. 14)*

In the letters to the editor, the contributors lamented the formation of a quarantine nightclub: "We certainly agree, in view of the establishment of a night club in the 'Garden of Eden,' that the name of that retreat should be changed" (ibid., p.18). Echoing the continued bantering between Adelaide and Melbourne came this song contribution:

> When the locked-up train leaves for the west
> And the dull stay in Melbourne is o'er,
> Though the night may be long,
> And the gargle stuff strong.
> I'll forget that the train trip's a bore.
> Far away where the stud sheep should roam.
> And the harvesters sleep when they're home.
> We shall sink down to rest,
> Thanks to this Spanish pest,
> In our quarantine home in South Aus
> *(Normal, 1919, p.2)*

* * *

There have also been various inclusions of the 1918 influenza in 21st-century popular culture and literature, from the sanitised sweep of the flu in *Downton Abbey* to *Twilight* where Edward Cullen is only saved from the flu by turning into a vampire. Notable Australian children's author Jackie French also used the stories from her grandmother to write *Horace the Baker's Horse* (2015) about her experience during the 1918 influenza for a younger, modern audience.

In an article by Andrew Stephens in the *Sydney Morning Herald* he reviewed the renewed interest in 'plague' literature, from Shakespeare's early life in Stratford-upon-Avon—when, in 1564, the plague killed 1 in 4—to Emily St John Mandel's work *Station Eleven* (2014) about a modern plague in Canada, and Melbourne author Steven Amsterdam's *Things We Didn't See Coming* (2009), a collection of short stories about disaster with an underlying premise of hope. All these modern examples capture the same essence of Shakespeare's claim, that despite the hopelessness many might feel during the far-reaching illness, this too shall pass.

With no comparable world-wide tragedy to contend with COVID-19 and to relegate it as a shadow trauma as occurred in the post-war pandemic, it will be interesting to observe how the pandemic of 2020–2022 is dealt with in literature and creative outputs in the coming years. Will it be variously overshadowed, blocked and incorporated into life as the 1918 influenza was, or will it provide a creative jolt for writers and creatives to re-think their place in the world and to appreciate the fleeting nature of 'healthy' life and the little things all of us took for granted before this occurred?

* * *

While very little is 'good' about enduring a bout of enforced isolation, from these examples, the benefit of perspective is clear. When one is restricted to a neighbourhood, a house, a room, or a head, it prompts an awareness of the simplicity of things. We may not be able to cross borders to visit family or attend conferences in Finland, though this slowing down has highlighted the importance and beauty of the simple things; of the companionship of a snail and its preference for envelope paper as a nightly entree or the need to go for a walk to clear our heads and accept that some days no words will arrive.

It is interesting as well that this chapter focusing on sickness is tinged with an overwhelmingly positive tone, from Bailey's companionship with the snail to the Adelaide detainees' poems and performances and the overall glass is half-full mentality. The perspective of isolation and illness in this instance also reflects much of what has been occurring in Australia and around the world in relation to the arts and humanities. While The Arts might not be essential in the way a doctor or supermarket worker is in current circumstances, the ability to consume, produce and reflect on the world through what we read, what we listen to and what we watch is more important than ever.

References

Arnold, C (2018). *Pandemic 1918: The Story of the Deadliest Influenza in History*. Michael O'Mara Books.

Barnes, J, & Kinsella, J (eds) (2009). *The Penguin Henry Lawson Short Stories*. Penguin Books.

Bauby, J-D (1998). *The Diving Bell and the Butterfly: A Memoir of Life in Death*. Fourth Estate.

Boochani, B (2018). *No Friend but the Mountains: Writing from Manus Prison* (trans. O Tofighian). Picador.

Brueggemann, BJ (2000). "Writing insight": Deafness and autobiography. *American Quarterly*, 52(2), 316–321.

Camus, A (1991 [1955]) *The Myth of Sisyphus and Other Essays* (trans. J O'Brien). Vintage Books.

Camus, A (1947). *The Plague* (trans. R Buss). Penguin Classics.

Cixous, H (1998). *Stigmata: Escaping Texts*. Routledge.

Couser, GT (1997). *Recovering Bodies Illness, Disability, and Life Writing*. University of Wisconsin Press.

Couser, GT (2011). Introduction: disability and life writing. *Journal of Literary & Cultural Disability Studies*, 5(3), 229–241.

Defoe, D (2003 [1722]). *A Journal of the Plague Year*. Penguin.

Dyson, W (1919). *Poems: In Memory of a Wife Who Died*. Cecil Palmer.

Eaves, W (2020). Should I stay or should I go? *Times Literary Supplement*, 15 May. Retrieved from www.the-tls.co.uk/articles/daniel-defoes-journal-of-a-plague-year-essay-will-eaves.

Jackson, A, & Brooks, D (2016). Editorial. *Southerly*, 76(2), 6–8.

Larsen, M (2019). The Great Picnic: 100 years since the Spanish Flu in Adelaide. Retrieved from https://blogs.adelaide.edu.au/special-collections/2019/07/10/the-great-picnic-100-years-since-the-spanish-flu-in-adelaide (accessed 2 April 2020).

Lovecraft, HP (1985 [1922]). *Herbert West: Reanimator*. Necronomicon PR.

Normal (1919). *Normal: Souvenir of the Quarantine Camp, Jubilee Oval, Adelaide, Feb. 26th–Mar. 5th, 1919.* Retrieved from https://nla.gov.au/nla.obj-52793464/view?partId=nla.obj-93243235.

Outka, E (2014). "Wood for the coffins ran out": Modernism and the shadowed afterlife of the influenza pandemic. *Modernism/Modernity* (Baltimore, MD), 21(4), 937–960. (doi:10.1353/mod.2014.0099)

Outka, E (2020). How pandemics seep into literature. Retrieved from www.theparisreview.org/blog/2020/04/08/how-pandemics-seep-into-literature (accessed 10 December 2020).

Porter, KA (2012 [1939]). *Pale Horse, Pale Rider.* Penguin.

Sontag, S (1978). *Illness as Metaphor.* Picador.

Stephens, A (2020). From Shakespeare and beyond, plague tales offer a glimpse of hope. *Sydney Morning Herald*, 3 April. Retrieved from www.smh.com.au/culture/books/from-shakespeare-and-beyond-plague-tales-offer-a-glimpse-of-hope-20200327-p54en2.html.

Stubbs, B (2016). A different view. *Southerly*, 76(2), 128–142.

Taylor, T (2018). The 1918 influenza pandemic affected the whole world. Could it happen again? Retrieved from www.abc.net.au/news/health/2018-04-13/flu-pandemic-1918-what-happened-and-could-it-happen-again/9601986 (accessed 15 February 2021).

Tilley, H (2017). *Blindness and Writing: From Wordsworth to Gissing.* Cambridge: Cambridge University Press.

Tink, A (2016). Deafness: A key to Lawson's writing. *Southerly*, 76 (2), 141–154.

Tova Bailey, E (2010). *The Sound of a Wild Snail Eating.* Text Publishing.

Turner, E (1919). Juliet in quarantine. *The Bulletin*, 40(2041) (27 March), 30.

White, J (2020). Silence is my habitat. In J Gildersleeve (ed.), *The Routledge Companion to Australian Literature.* Taylor and Francis, pp. 243–253.

4

INCARCERATION

Journalist Peter Greste smuggled out letters written on toilet paper from his Cairo jail cell and stuffed them inside his dirty socks. Iranian writer and activist Behrouz Boochani wrote an entire book on smuggled mobile phones secreted in his mattress from within the confines of his Manus Island prison. And Jean Lee operated the only journalism service from within the hermit kingdom of North Korea as the Associated Press's Pyongyang bureau chief.

There are many examples of writing as it relates to different types of incarceration and confinement that can allow us to find deeper meaning and different articulations of optimism through creativity. The writer/prisoner's ability to travel in a more proximate, humanist sense is also something the average reader (and average travel writer) can appreciate. While we have now had the chance to consider the pathological tourism which existed around the world pre-pandemic, the ability of those incarcerated to embody spiritual and imaginative travel, while also considering space in a similar manner to Xavier de Maistre did in the 18th century allows us to engage with their locations, the reasons for their incarceration and how it impacts us now as armchair voyeurs and travellers ourselves. The writing from the incarcerated also permits readers to travel inside with them, thus being able to better understand their situations.

There are many elements of the previous chapters that I can access and engage with directly. I know very well what it is to be one who travels frequently across oceans and into cities on different continents. I know what it is to reflect and look deeper at how we can rethink the significance of travel and what the notion of travel means in a world when we can't. I also know, as many of us now do through the pandemic of 2020–2022, what it is to be confined, to be isolated from loved ones and to live with uncertainty due to illness. With both examples I also know how important writing can be as a way to think more deeply about confinement and to come to terms with it in some creative way.

DOI: 10.4324/9781003243267-4

With this chapter on incarceration, however, this is something I cannot do directly. I have no experience of being locked up. I don't know what it is to be stateless, to be targeted and to be incarcerated. And I can't draw from personal experience on how important writing can be as a lighthouse for those submerged in the darkness of a prison sentence. As this book is written partly in response to, and during, the COVID-19 pandemic, and today as I write the Victorian capital of Melbourne has just overtaken Buenos Aires as the city which has spent the most time under lockdown in the world during the pandemic and its citizens are onto day 246, hence this experience is maybe something that Victorians, and the people of Melbourne in particular, have a firmer grasp on.

* * *

While once the determination of more traditional imprisonment was to look at the interned person as an object of penal domination (Beasley, 2015), Foucault began the mapping of the shift in the 18th and 19th centuries of the purpose of imprisonment, with the notion that any prisoner can be transformed through work and education. As hopeful as this is, the role of writing as an act of defiance, as an organiser of time and as a window to allow travel outside the walls of confinement is clear. Writing while incarcerated can also demonstrate a fortified self-image and assist with the reduction of stress through learning and practising the process of self-reflection (Palmer et al., 1994).

Despite this ideal of writing acting as rehabilitation, it is obviously not something that many prisoners have been able to practice freely. Notwithstanding this, there is a rich contribution from incarcerated people on writing and the space it fills during their imprisonment and there is something we can hold onto as writers and readers in the COVID era to better understand the context and role of writing within this form of isolation.

While there are many historically notable incarceration narratives: *Papillon, The Gulag Archipelago, The Long Walk to Freedom* and Gramsci's *Prison Notebooks* from being locked up in 1930s fascist Italy, Serge's *Men in Prison* and Berkman's 1912 book *Prison Memoirs of an Anarchist,* it is worth considering how writing during the incarceration of renowned international leaders and visionaries played a key role in maintaining their drive to keep going, and their hope that there would be eventual change.

While the incarceration of Nelson Mandela, who was imprisoned for 27 years in South Africa from 1962 until 1990, is well known, there is less focus on his writing during this period. Mandela wrote hundreds of letters during his 10,000 incarcerated days. He would write about the importance of attitude to his wife Winnie after more than six years inside, "Remember that hope is a powerful weapon even when all else is lost" (Mandela, 2018) he replied to her. In his letters Mandela reflected on the death of his son in a car accident in 1969 and he tried to console his children from his cell as best he could, "Zindzi says her heart is sore because I am not at home and wants to know when I will come back. I do not know, my darlings, when I will return" (ibid.). He would write of the clarity he would strive for and the commitment to the development of his inner self while enduring long bouts of solitary confinement. In 1976, Mandela also wrote specifically of the importance of writing while he was in his cell in another letter to Winnie:

> It's always given me plenty of satisfaction and joy to write to you. I sincerely don't know whether you'll ever get this particular one nor those of July 18, Aug 1 and 18 and, if you do, when that'll be. Nonetheless, the act of writing to you at this moment removes all the tensions and impurities in my feelings and thoughts. It's the only time I ever feel that some day in the future it'll be possible for humanity to produce saints who will really be upright and venerable, inspired in everything they do by genuine love for humanity and who'll serve all humans selflessly.
>
> *(Mandela, 2018)*

In Mandela's memoir *Long Walk to Freedom* he details the importance of writing his story in his own words, as an activity that would transport him beyond the walls. During the long nights he would write in concealed darkness to travel beyond his prison cell, and as a means to record what had happened to him in his many years before and during his incarceration.

In the lead up to his sixtieth birthday Mandela planned to begin writing his memoir so that the struggle of his life, and the cause he fought for would be remembered and would continue to inspire young freedom fighters. Complicating this though was the proscription on the writing or images of banned and imprisoned individuals; even an editor could join him in jail if caught receiving or publishing any of his writing. He would write during the night and sleep during the day to better avoid detection. Mandela enlisted the help of his fellow inmates Walter Sisulu and Ahmed Kathrada to help him edit, proof-read, and ultimately hide the manuscript. To ensure the safety of the memoir they would get another inmate, Laloo Chiba, to re-write Mandela's chapters into his own microscopic shorthand to better conceal it before the book was smuggled out by Mac Maharaj who was soon to be released. Mandela wrote of the experience:

> I relived my experiences as I wrote about them. Those nights, as I wrote in silence, I could once again experience the sights and sounds of my youth in Qunu and Mqhekezweni; the excitement and fear of coming to Johannesburg; the tempests of the Youth League; the endless delays of the Treason Trial; the drama of Rivonia. It was like a waking dream and I attempted to transfer it to paper as simply and truthfully as I could.
>
> *(Mandela, 2013, p.477)*

There was a further complication, however, as even though Maharaj had the full shorthand document on the outside, they still had Mandela's original 500-page memoir on the inside, which they had to dispose of. Mandela and his inner circle of friends split the book into three sections, wrapped them in plastic and concealed the pages in old cocoa tins. "We did the only thing we thought we could do: we buried it in the courtyard in the garden" (ibid., p.478) wrote Mandela. This plan worked for a time, until they realised that there were maintenance works going on in the yard where they had buried the memoir. The political prisoners managed to surreptitiously dig up two of the sections and dispose of them, though, not the largest pile, which was lodged underneath a pipe in the soil. The warders noticed Mandela's erratic behaviour and the final section was discovered. Mandela and Sisulu lost their study privileges for 4 years because of this, though the shorthand manuscript eventually arrived in London with Maharaj. The text, though, was not published until much later, when it formed a large part of Mandela's memoir.

The ability to write and send messages out into the world was also seen in another South African prison, though by India's spiritual leader. While Mahatma Gandhi is also known for his campaigning for equal rights and against racial discrimination, it was also in South Africa, where Gandhi lived for 21 years from the late 19th century where he was imprisoned four times for leading protests against discrimination. As he returned to India and began to rile against the injustice in his own country, he was also imprisoned. He wrote many letters, though the most notable is said to be the typed letter from his house arrest where he called for his movement to a regular jail:

> It is unthinkable that when India's millions are suffering from preventable starvation and thousands are dying of it, thousands of men and women should be kept in detention on mere suspicion when their energy and the expense incurred in keeping them under duress could at this critical time be usefully employed in relieving distress ... the huge place in which I am being detained with a large guard around me I hold to be a waste of public funds. I should be quite content to pass my days in any prison.
>
> *(Gandhi, 2006, p.510)*

This was also a key moment in the identification of Gandhi as a selfless and determined leader and the move for an independent India, which Gandhi would achieve four years later.

In 2019 more than 200 inmates in Narsinghpur Central Jail in India took Gandhi's lead and wrote letters to promote positive change. The prisoners wrote to their victims' families from jail, hoping to create a dialogue and a sense of openness through writing. Their aim was to allow the families to "hate the sin, not the sinner" (Express News Service, 2019) through their letter writing.

* * *

While the COVID-19 pandemic has been tumultuous on many fronts, the emergence of the Black Lives Matter movement has also taken hold throughout cities in the Western world. The message of Dr Martin Luther King Jr about civil rights, equality and oppression has come to the fore once again as protests, marches and action are precipitated. There is also something to observe from Dr King in relation to his writing in confinement with his 'A letter from Birmingham Jail' written in 1963 after he was imprisoned for participating in non-violent protests against segregation in the south of the United States. His letter was a response to the public statement from eight white religious leaders who criticised the protests as "unwise and untimely" (King, 2018, p.1).

King's response to the injustice, as he sat in a narrow cell in Alabama, echo the messages of the BLM movement today, and the highlighting of the plight of persecuted and ignored people more broadly. King wrote that "whatever affects one directly affects all indirectly" (King, 2018, p.1).

King used his time in isolation to write, calmly and clearly of their reasons for protest, for non-violent action and to emphasise examples of injustice, "what else can one do when he is alone in a narrow jail cell, other than write long letters, think long thoughts and pray long prayers?" (King, 2018, p.6). When responding to the clergy's call for them to wait and be patient, King wrote: "It has been a tranquilizing thalidomide, relieving the emotional stress for a moment, only to give birth to an ill-formed infant of frustration" (ibid., p.2).

King's long letter was copied via mimeograph. It was published across the country and presented to Congress as a marker for positive change.

All three of these men would have enormous social, political, and cultural impact on their communities, and it was in part through their writing that they maintained and persevered with the hope they contained for change. In the 21st century this desire to use writing while incarcerated to affect positive change remains the same.

* * *

The most notorious example in recent memory of writing and confinement as it relates to incarceration—and Australian culpability—is that of Behrouz Boochani. The tall, inquisitive man was a poet and a journalist in Iran, born in Ilam in Kurdistan before he studied journalism in Tehran under the backdrop of the Iran–Iraq war. The pride of his Kurdish heritage saw him targeted when he was the editor of a local magazine, *Werya*, and he was subsequently arrested and interrogated for his ongoing support of the Kurdish cause.

Boochani wrote that he always considered becoming a Peshmerga, a revolutionary in the mountains, though the power of the pen drew him to the city to assume his battle in a non-violent manner. He continued to write about Kurdish independence even as his colleagues were incarcerated for their similar pro-Kurdish stance. The magazine's offices were raided and Boochani was told that unless he fled, he would also end up in jail. So, he ran. He ended up in Indonesia, as so many fleeing persecution in the Middle East do, and a smuggler convinced Boochani that he could get him safe passage to Australia. He paid $5000, though the first boat sank at sea. With his second attempt, their boat was lost on the Indian

Ocean, drifting for a week. While he was lost and floating on the open ocean, then Prime Minister Kevin Rudd uttered the infamous statement that would change the course of Boochani's life, and so many other asylum seekers' lives:

> From this point forward asylum seekers who arrive in Australia by boat will be sent to Papua New Guinea for processing and resettlement. The rules have changed. If you come by boat, you will never permanently live in Australia.
>
> *(Rudd, 2013)*

After a period interred on Christmas Island where he was dressed in ill-fitting yellow polyester clothes and flip-flops, he was flown to Manus Island, where he would be confined for the next six years.

The scenes that Boochani wrote about in his book *No Friend but the Mountains* are horrific as he detailed the pressure within humid, fetid tropical prison alongside his observations and the strain of the seemingly unending ordeal. We read of his struggle to cope, to see an end to the torture and to find hope while he is imprisoned. One of the clear methods Boochani used to pull himself through the experience and to capture it for others to understand, was by writing it down—in a deft combination of reportage, poetry, and academic immersion. He wrote of arriving on Manus Island in a place that is so hot, humid and fecund that it is suffocating, "It seems as though the jungle is striving to seize all surrounding areas" (Boochani, 2018, p.103), he noted the pointless administration forms, the fat Australians doused in sunscreen, the terrified Manusians working for them, and his bewilderment at what was occurring, "Can it be that I sought asylum in Australia only to be exiled to a place I know nothing about?" (ibid., p.107). He even wrote that he would be prepared to get back on that Indonesian fishing boat if he were allowed. The story he tells is disturbing, though the act of writing captures this important moment and the inhumanity of the Australian Government by attempting to shuffle its problems offshore.

Boochani delivered his manuscript in short, encoded messages via WhatsApp, demonstrating the commitment and creativity involved in the production of his story—just as with Jean-Dominique Bauby in *The Diving Bell and the Butterfly*, the ingenuity encountered behind each of their 'closed doors' allowed for both these important stories to reach the wider world.

In an interview with the ABC's *Australian Story*, Boochani said that he "didn't feel safe to write it on paper" (McDermott, 2019), and so he resorted to using smuggled phones to deliver the account of his imprisonment, with the devices hidden in a cavity that he created in his mattress.

Boochani interspersed the narrative of what was happening with his own poetry, showing us in his writing that even as the madness of the island increased, the softness of those brief moments after the sun lost its bite, or when he could steal a few quiet moments with a cigarette were what kept him going for the six torturous years.

Boochani decided that creativity, writing, and imagination provided escape, and allowed him to see through the windows as if there were no bars. There is a meta-narrative within Boochani's writing—there is the book on his time in Manus, and then there is also the writing of the escape that writing provided for him while imprisoned:

> the only people who can overcome and survive all the suffering inflicted by the prison are those who exercise creativity. That is, those who can trace the outlines of hope using the melodic humming and visions from beyond the prison fences and the beehives we live in.
>
> *(Boochani, 2018, p.128)*

Boochani demonstrated the use of the kyriarchal system with his writing of the experience on Manus. He defines kyriarchal system as "a web of intersecting oppressions (racism, sexism, colonialism et cetera) that maintains society's dominant hierarchies" (ibid.), this framing allowed Boochani to make some sense of the experience as he saw it, around the constant oppression and belittling of the inmates. And so, there is a double reading of his book, of the narrative as it immerses us deeper and deeper into his experiences and the helplessness of being incarcerated, punctuated with stanzas of his poetic observations. These are gulps of air, yet still tormented and visceral, as the perspective descends further:

> The prison is in the middle of a clenched fist/
> Now loosening, now tightening/
> On the verge of exploding/
> Then, all of a sudden, balance is re-established.
>
> *(Boochani, 2018, p.175)*

As we read his story, the anguish and frustration of the perspective is clear and as the writing continues, the tangled roots of the experience emerge—often centred around the toilets, the stench and the control the guards exercise over them. In *The Oldman/Generator* chapter, Boochani detailed how, with the push of a button, the world the detainees clung to was torn from their grasp. Is it just the temperamental burps of an old generator in the tropics, with "Poles and pipes of rusty metal" (ibid., p.177)? Or is it purposely turned off, with the press of a button, Boochani wondered, to demonstrate how their fate rested in the guard's hands? They are tired, itchy, confused. When the lights turn off in a blackout and the water supply is temperamental, there is confusion among the inmates and a rush to the toilets. "The smell is so vile that one feels ashamed to be part of the human species" (ibid., p.179). And then the lights turn on. It is an exercise of control.

What makes this even more affecting is the realisation that he wrote this with his thumbs—on a secreted phone and sent these encrypted messages out to his confidants: refugee advocate Moones Mansoubi, Janet Galbraith, who established the 'Writing Through Fences' group dedicated to giving a voice to incarcerated refugees, Arnold Zable, who championed Behrouz's story and helped amplify it to the world, academic and artist Kirrily Jordan, and Omid Tofighian. As Boochani wrote in the foreword discussion with the translator, Tofighian, "I think it's inevitable that for years and years to come I'll end up opening critical spaces for engaging with the phenomenon of Manus Prison" (Boochani, 2018, p.xxvii).

Beyond his book, Behrouz was also able to continue telling the story of Manus—as journalist and witness for *The Saturday Paper* and the *Guardian* in particular—as his writing charted the reality on the island that the Australian Government hoped to conceal.

In *The Saturday Paper* Boochani reminded the Australians reading his notes of their greater importance, and of the uncomfortable reality of what Australian readers only appreciate from a distance: "We have reminded a majority of the Australian public that throughout their history they have only ever imagined that their democracy and freedom has been created on the basis of principles of humanity" (Boochani, 2017).

Just as with Mandela, Gandhi, and King before him, Boochani's opposition to his incarceration is a symbol for his unwillingness to relent or accept the hopelessness that the Australian Government tries to stain the prison with. "Our resistance is the spirit that haunts Australia. Our resistance is a new manifesto for humanity and love" (Boochani, 2017).

Part of Boochani's thesis is to examine how writing can provide space, relief, and direction for his otherwise directionless experience. This same analysis was also taken up previously by Jean Améry, an Austrian Jew, who was part of the Belgian resistance movement and incarcerated in Auschwitz for a year. He wrote *At the Mind's Limits* (Améry, 2009) partly to examine how intellectuals and creative people found meaning within the camps, and if this sensibility assisted them to cope with their imprisonment.

Améry concluded that this intellectual engagement was not enough, and he envied the working class and those without the same expectations or cultural awareness. Despite this, in a later analysis of Améry's writing, Magdalena Zolkos concluded that for Améry, "the act of writing becomes that of resistance and a reclamation of voice and language in the face of the fascistic powers aimed at expelling, silencing, and eliminating the 'undesirables'" (Zolkos, 2019, p.57). As Jeff Sparrow beautifully wrote in the *Sydney Review of Books*, "where Améry concludes that culture provides no solution, Boochani insists that the key to surviving 'all the suffering inflicted by the prison' lies in the exercise of creativity" (Sparrow, 2018).

Sparrow continued:

> Boochani describes how literature facilitated precisely the transcendence that Améry sought but couldn't find in poetry. "[W]hen I was writing," he says, "I

> was completely free … those moments were the most exciting … because I found myself out of the prison as a free man."
>
> *(Sparrow, 2018)*

Boochani saw the role of writing as one that saved and preserved him for the six years:

> Previously, at any time I expected a guard would attack my room. That's one of the reasons why I did not publish anything under my real name for more than two years. I did not feel safe and for a while I even thought that the system might kill me. At that time, when I was unknown, the system could have killed me in the way that it killed Reza Barati … Being known, perhaps, and my work being recognised and supported by organisations and other thinkers and artists perhaps gives me an element of protection.
>
> *(Zable, 2018)*

As Boochani detailed in the foreword to *No Friend but the Mountains*, Janet Galbraith was instrumental in the voyage that saw his writing published, the story of Manus Island carried across the world and his eventual resettlement in New Zealand when he was broken free by the plan to allow him to visit the 'Word Writers Festival' in Christchurch. A visa is not required for speakers, so he was secreted out of Papua New Guinea in 2019 and has since settled in New Zealand.

Galbraith is the founder of 'Writing Through Fences', which is a writing collective aimed at giving a voice to people previously or still incarcerated in Australia's immigration detention centres. The collective's aim is to facilitate creativity, collaboration and resistance and they have a variety of mentor spaces, project pages, translation services and English instruction for writers, artists, and musicians.

Boochani wrote of the role of Galbraith in giving a voice to these voiceless people using poetry and poetic language to create distance between the experience and the subsequent writing of it, "For me it was a way to send out words and know that someone was reading them" (Boochani, 2020). Boochani also noted how being creative while incarcerated helped him and his fellow detainees survive and to realise that they do have a voice they can use.

If Boochani's case is notable because of the impact Australian political decisions had on him and many others, it is the similar effect of external politics which determined the fate of another high-profile case of incarceration involving an Australian writer.

* * *

The journalist Peter Greste's case is now infamous. In 2013 he was working for Al Jazeera English as a foreign correspondent.

This was just a placeholder gig. He wasn't there to break any stories or push any boundaries, he was simply holding the fort for the Cairo bureau until the permanent replacement arrived. Greste was based in the Marriott Hotel and after the tension between the government and the Muslim Brotherhood (MB), and the government's blaming the MB for a series of explosions and protests in the city, Greste was keeping a low profile—only doing 'normal journalism', nothing that would place him and his colleagues close to the attention of the government and their crackdown on foreign journalists. But then on 29 December 2013 came an aggressive knock at his door. A group of men from the Interior Ministry burst through his door, confiscated his devices, and marched him back through the lobby of the hotel, under arrest. As his colleague Mohamed Fahmy arrived and spoke to the captors in Arabic, they realised that this wasn't a simple intimidation ploy or a stunt to receive a pay-off, and they were transported to a cold, stone police station in Cairo that stank of stale urine and tobacco. Greste and Fahmy were bundled into a cell with nine others, before being transferred to a National Security prison where they would learn that this wasn't going to be something they could get out of quickly and easily.

In the affecting books about his ordeal, *Freeing Peter* and *The First Casualty*, Greste's story is told as he was buried further and further into the Egyptian legal system. Reflecting a different way of approaching the theme of writing and isolation, *Freeing Peter* is co-written with Peter from the recollections and journal entries of Greste's parents and two brothers outside the walls of the prison as they lobbied and came to terms with his incarceration.

As a foreign correspondent Greste was no stranger to risk and dangerous situations—his colleague Kate Peyton was shot and killed when they were in Somalia, and he had reported from Afghanistan, Colombia, and many other dangerous locations around the world. This was different though. He was stuck.

Greste wrote of the reaction to hearing the tales of migration, war and struggle of his parents who had arrived in Australia as Latvian immigrants, "I want to have stories. I want my life to be built of stories" (Greste et al., 2016, p.29) and as they were interrogated, moved to different cells and faced with the seriousness of the situation, pressed in close enough to his cell mate that he could feel the thumping of his pulse, Greste had become the story.

As Greste's story developed further and he began to endure the now infamous 400 days in Egyptian prisons, the role of writing became more prominent. At first it was the scraps of paper given by cell mates so he could take notes about conversations, and later while in solitary confinement in Tora prison he adopted a regime of exercise, meditation, writing and reading to help him endure the time. Beyond the push-ups, scissor kicks, and sit-ups, he would write in his notebook and read Fernando Pessoa's *The Book of Disquiet*, a meditation about the boredom of an office worker's life in Lisbon, to give meaning to his days.

Greste began writing letters as a form of record and clarification, to capture his thoughts and to raise awareness of what was occurring with his struggle as the power of the incarceration became more obvious. He found the small things precious: the winter sun, the books secreted into his cell and the pen and pad he could write with. These small mercies seemed nearly as important as the freedom he craved from the insulation of the flaking cell. Greste's letters were taken from prison by a contact and eventually published online via Facebook as the first ripples of the injustice were felt. His letters would raise the profile of his case to become internationally notorious for the corruption, political protectionism and farce Greste would find himself in the middle of.

Greste tapped into the lessons he had learned practising Vipassana meditation to separate out his senses and to tease out the moments of his day. He identified the sounds of the rubber thongs on inmates, the *click-clack* of officers' boots and the feeling of the sun at midday that warmed his chest, even if initially "writing didn't come easily" (Greste et al., 2016, p. 55). In these moments he also embodied something of Xavier de Maistre's vertical travel and the nostalgia it prompted. The trees thrashing in the wind outside his cell would remind him of a trip to Argentina to learn hang gliding. And then he was able to teleport into the experience and re-live, "the freedom of the air, the thrill of the lift-off and the glide" (ibid., p.46) from his travels.

When his brother Andrew arrived in Cairo and he was given a letter to smuggle out of Tora, as reading and writing materials were contraband in his early imprisonment, he also understood the power and importance of writing in Greste's conditions. The notes were written on toilet paper and often stuffed inside dirty socks and laundry bags to escape detection. This would be a constant for Greste during his stay—passing on letters, shopping lists and notes hidden in dirty clothes and washing bags to connect him with the outside world. His brothers Mike and Andrew would learn the same procedure—smuggling in writing for him from friends and family so he could have a connection to the outside world and the progress of his case.

As time passed and the frustration mounted, Greste struggled to find meaning in his incarceration. This lived experience, he reflected on, should give him the ultimate inside knowledge as a journalist and one who writes about other people's struggles for a living. "Some literature seems to glamorise prison, make it heroic, give it meaning" (Greste et al., 2016, p.104), but what it didn't tell him, was about the utter boredom of the experience as the days extended to weeks and then months. As Foucault wrote in *Discipline and Punish*, "Time penetrates the body and with it all the meticulous controls of power" (Foucault, 1995, p.152). Greste realised that writing would be his way of maintaining what control he could during his incarceration, it would allow him to transport himself beyond his cell, to be with his family and to fill his days with the things he would rather be doing.

After the verdict and the seven-year sentence was passed down at the trial, the improved conditions at Masraa prison allowed Greste easier access to reading and writing materials. Despite his dark cell, still populated with 21 inmates and the constant drone of the communal television, Greste noted that he had a compelling need to write and to record the details of their incarceration so that it would help their cause as those from the outside read it. It also allowed Greste to take refuge in his profession as a storyteller while permitting him his own space away from his co-accused and the others in the cells with him.

To find a deeper connection with the isolation and the importance of writing, one of the writers Greste read in prison was Viktor Frankel, who wrote *Man's Search for Meaning* from within the Nazi concentration camps. Greste wrote of Frankel's influence and the belief that he who has a *why* can endure any *how*, and writing it down was a way of finding the *why*. Greste wrote that by putting it in a letter that was then published it gave that '*why*' a lot more relevance, significance, and meaning (Greste, 2017).

The creativity and expression while confined didn't just manifest itself in Greste's writing. One thing he took up, which many people during the COVID-19 pandemic understand for its simple joy, is baking bread. Greste would get lost in cooking in his makeshift kitchen with the spices and recipes he could procure along with small packets of seeds smuggled in by his uncle Ojars that he would plant in a bag of soil he would leave in the sun. The seeds would eventually sprout into chives, mint, and coriander to add to his meals. He wrote of the creative hobby he would practise inside—from nurturing yeast starters to scrounging ingredients to make flavoured loaves for his cellmates and its importance to his incarcerated existence.

Eventually, on a visit from Ojars, he is given the most unusual, but joyful thing—the course material for his external International Relations Masters degree at Griffith University. The staff at Griffith compiled 13 kilograms of reading and course material, and delivered it to the Australian Embassy, who then transported it to Tora prison. The university sent through numerous emails with attachments to the embassy and the embassy would print out a box full of papers. He would get an embassy visit every two weeks, so he would complete his assignments and pass them on to the embassy staff, they'd scan it, email it, and forward along to the lecturer. Greste eventually completed his studies, though his imprisonment continued.

In the cold Egyptian winter Greste wrote in his diary, "The whole mess feels so stupid, caught by a combination of bureaucratic red tape and procedure, political gutlessness, and a lack of genuine concern for human beings" (Greste et al., 2016, p.253). He noted that he made fish soup for dinner, and it lifted his spirits, and that maybe he should consider a hunger strike to prompt some action. It would be his last journal entry. The next day he was a free man. He received the news that he had 30 minutes to gather his things, so he stuffed his few clothes in a bag, gathered his writing and outstanding assignments, and was released.

Peter Greste is now a professor of Journalism at the University of Queensland.

* * *

There are also intriguing perspectives of writing and incarceration other than the prisoners. In 2018 Shane Bauer wrote *American Prisons* posing as a guard to allow him to look at the privatisation of the American penal system, and in 1988, with *Newjack*, immersive journalist Ted Conover wanted to understand what the reality of America's prison system was like from the inside. He discounted the option of entering as an inmate, and instead enlisted in the Department of Correctional Services' officer training program and was eventually employed in New York's Sing Sing prison. Conover's rationale was that with prisons in the news constantly, with the enormous cost, the stereotypes of inmates and guards, and the increasing numbers of people incarcerated, he wrote, "it seemed to me that their operations should be completely transparent" (Conover, 2000 [1988], p.17), yet he knew if he went in as a journalist, he would be given PR spin. What he witnessed was more than he had considered initially, "It was an experience of living with fear—fear of inmates, as individuals and as a mob, and fear of our own capacity to fuck up" (ibid., p.95).

Conover was living the discipline and regulations echoed by Foucault. He realised how much this was a microcosm of a totalitarian society, but also how these rules didn't always work when applied to real people who were facing decades locked up. He learned that contraband wasn't just drugs, alcohol, and weapons, but also chewing gum, shoes worth more than $50 and even being caught in possession of more than 14 newspapers. The shades of grey were the most obvious lesson Conover learned in his first months as a guard. More surprising was how much responsibility those in uniform were enlisted with, despite being underpaid, undertrained, and poorly resourced. Conover hid a small notebook in his breast pocket, and he would scribble rushed notes in between jobs and purge all his observations from his memory into his writing books or at home on his computer as soon as his shift finished. He would recall the veracity of his observations, of being spat at, of checking prisoners for stab marks, or working out the office politics before they would fade. The pressure of the writing also took on new meaning. As his experience expanded, he would not tell anyone what he was doing, his friends and family had no idea and even his wife would only be told scant details. Writing it down became his only outlet, and like the inmates before him, it became his way of making sense of the incarceration. In the aftermath of *Newjack*, Conover's writing about prison from the inside became contraband in Sing Sing before it was redacted so they could read about his observations of their prison. In the end, Conover's experience left him with a strange taste in his mouth, as he realised that it is both the prisoners and the prison guards who leave the institution worse off than when they arrived.

* * *

A further interesting interpretation of writing and confinement comes from Jean Lee, the former Associated Press journalist. She was tasked in 2011 with setting up a North Korea bureau in Pyongyang. She was the first American journalist allowed to be stationed there and it was the first time outsiders could get a perspective of the country from within. "I had to relinquish my cell phone", Lee said in an interview with the Korea Society (Lee, 2015), and even though she tried to hide her iPhone, it was discovered, and she was cut off from any independent communication with the outside world. "I had no way to contact anyone, who memorises phone numbers anymore?", she said (ibid.). On government organised trips she was with 'guides' 24 hours a day and everything was predetermined. Lee said that North Koreans are very closed off from the outside world and they are raised to believe that America is the enemy, so this presented a unique opportunity to write about the country while being 'locked in'. As Lee travelled around the country, she was also able to see behind the closed doors of North Korea beyond the orchestrated press junkets for foreign journalists in the past. Lee would not allow her work to be reviewed or censored, and as a result she would find herself in homes, factories, farms, and military academies—still chaperoned by government officials—though the response to this access would often be that she was the first American, and the first foreign journalist that they'd ever met. This allowed nuance, perspective, and honesty in the representation of North Korea in a way it hadn't been allowed before, coming from this ground-up perspective. She would see how disabled people were integrated into the workforce as barbers and hair-dressers; she witnessed the treatment of war veterans; and she discovered American beer sitting on the shelves of Pyongyang's supermarkets. Lee's period writing from the isolation of North Korea revealed many of the oddities of the country, but also the examples of normal life that were able to be captured when one had the chance to look closer.

* * *

What about writing and confinement from other contributors? How have those who weren't writers beforehand utilised writing while incarcerated?

The Australian literary journal *Westerly* embraced this opportunity with their 2018 edition exploring the many creative voices of South Australia. As part of this, the Life Sentences programme was created, and prisoners had the chance to write their stories and be published in a nationally acclaimed journal.

Dr Michael Savvas wrote about the impact of the program for *The Conversation*:

> What Life Sentences contributors wrote about was telling. Most entries directly related to what American criminologist Greshem Sykes called the "pains of imprisonment" in 1958. This wasn't surprising, and it is hoped writing about such pains was healing for the writers. What was more surprising was the number of entries *not* directly about imprisonment.
>
> *(Savvas, 2020)*

Jeremy Ryder of the Art by Prisoners programme wrote of the Life Sentences contribution:

> Some writing takes you far away from prison to childhood memories, to warmer, happier times and places. Others express the chaotic lives of those who cycle in and out of the system. Many of the stories take you deep into prison, to the smells and tastes, but also into the painful emotional world of

> people grappling with isolation, separation, addiction, trauma and, of course, one's status as a 'prisoner'. But within that dark world there is also light—strength, hope and humour. It is through this writing that we can get new perspectives on prison and of the lives of those incarcerated within them
>
> *(Cothren & Mead, 2018, p.33)*

Here is a selection from the Life Sentences edition in 2018:

Little Treasure

Gentle blue eyes
Sweet little smile
Growing up so fast
This is my child

Contagious little laugh
Temper so wild
My gorgeous little boy
This is my child

A beautiful miracle
A voice so mild
My darling little treasure
This is my child

I wish I could see him
It's been a while
Three years have passed
This is my child

He doesn't remember me
Or the love that I had
He has a brand new family
A new mum and dad
But I will never forget
His sweet little smile
My darling little boy
Is now their child

(2017/34 Female, 26, in Cothren & Mead, 2018, p.36)

* * *

In 2020, as part of the South Australian Living Artists Festival—run online due to COVID-19—the Life Sentences programme produced another collection of writing, though these seem much more poignant as readers can now only access the work remotely, the writing only 'set free' with the click of a mouse as people immerse in the digital exhibition.

In Victoria, the Torch does a similar thing, providing creative and artistic outlets for Indigenous offenders and ex-offenders through its various arts programmes to allow them to travel beyond their daily confinement:

> Every time that I pick the brush up and start painting, I'm not here anymore, I'm not in the jail. I'm actually in there, down the river and fishing and hunting and doing all those good things. It was an escape.
>
> *(Angus Abdullah (Noongar/Yamatji), in Torch, 2020)*

* * *

Writing behind the closed doors of prison seems more complex, understandably, than many other examples in this book. As we see with the diverse testimonies of Peter Greste, Martin Luther King, Behrouz Boochani, and Jean Lee among others, what it also demonstrates is that just as with the other examples in this book, the writing from within confinement allows for a sense of two-way travel. This is possible for both the inmates, who can transport themselves imaginatively to their home lives or into the story of their journey into the cell. Alongside this, the writing from the incarcerated also invites readers to travel in a manner that is not just novel for its ability to understand what Manus Island, Manaa prison, or Sing Sing look, smell, and feel like, but to also be transported into a space that allows for a greater sense of empathy for what they have endured. There is a need to document things so there is a record—of the journey to Christmas Island on a leaking boat, of the process of counting push ups to keep the mind and body active, and baking bread with smuggled herbs in Cairo, but there is also a need for the writers to document the impact this incarceration has internally. The writing is an important device that charts the onset of depression, the hallucinations borne from the oppressive heat in Manus and the kyriarchal system of oppression being forced on the prisoners. The fragility of all the writers here is clear, both subtextually and implicitly within the texts. What the writing does is to acknowledge the importance of the experience to give it space and legitimacy in a way that their incarceration would not.

The binding theme from writing within incarceration seems to be the kindling and sustaining of hope. Hope for change, hope for release, hope that someone will read their writing and be impacted.

It is a joyful thing that many of the cases of those who have written while incarcerated have found physical liberation, though one aspect that is clear from the writing of the incarcerated is that the ripple of its impact remains even if writing allows them to travel outwards for respite and release, and for readers to empathise and better understand the ordeal by momentarily venturing inside the walls with the writer.

References

Beasley, C (2015). Teaching behind bars: Challenges and solutions for creative writing classes in Prison. *TEXT: Journal of Writing and Writing Courses*, 19(2).

Améry, J (2009). *At the Mind's Limits*. Indiana University Press.

Boochani, B (2017). A letter from Manus Island. *The Saturday Paper*, 9–15 December. Retrieved from www.thesaturdaypaper.com.au/news/politics/2017/12/09/letter-manus-island/15127380005617#hrd (accessed 10 January 2021).

Boochani, B (2018). Manus Prison theory. *The Saturday Paper*, 11–17 August. Retrieved from www.thesaturdaypaper.com.au/opinion/topic/2018/08/11/manus-prison-theory/15339096006690#hrd (accessed 22 November 2020).

Boochani, B (2018). *No Friend but the Mountains: Writing from Manus Prison*. (translated by Omid Tofighian). Picador.

Boochani, B (2020). Writing through fences. *The Saturday Paper*, 19–25 September. Retrieved from www.thesaturdaypaper.com.au/culture/books/2020/09/19/writing-through-fences/160043760010433#hrd (accessed 30 September 2020).

Conover, T (2000 [1988]). *New Jack: Guarding Sing Sing*. Penguin.

Cothren, A & Mead, A (eds) (2018). South Australia. *Westerly*, special issue 6.

Express News Service (2019). Madhya Pradesh's convicted inmates write letters seeking forgiveness from victims. *The New Indian Express*, 4 November. Retrieved from www.newindianexpress.com/nation/2019/nov/04/madhya-pradeshs-convicted-inmates-write-letters-seeking-forgiveness-from-victims–2056787.html (accessed 20 November 2020).

Foucault, M (1995). *Discipline and Punish*. Vintage.

Gandhi, R (2006). *Mohandas: A True Story of a Man, His People, and an Empire*. Penguin.

Greste, P (2017). *First Casualty: A Memoir from the Frontlines of the Global War on Journalism*. Viking.

Greste, J, Greste, P, Greste, M, Greste, L, & Greste, A (2016). *Freeing Peter: How an Ordinary Family Fought an Extraordinary Battle*. Penguin.

King, ML, Jr (2018). *Letter from Birmingham Jail*. Penguin Classics.

Lee, J (2015). Opening Pyongyang: Korea and media perceptions with Jean H. Lee. 16 May. Retrieved from www.youtube.com/watch?v=oFynZllH3gc.

Mandela, N (2013). *Long Walk to Freedom*. Little Brown.

Mandela, N (2018). "Hope is a powerful weapon": Unpublished Mandela Prison letters. *New York Times*. Retrieved from www.nytimes.com/2018/07/06/opinion/sunday/nelson-mandela-unpublished-prison-letters-excerpts.html (accessed 1 October 2021).

McDermott, Q (2019). Behrouz Boochani's mission to change offshore detention laws using a smuggled mobile phone. Australian Story. Retrieved from www.abc.net.au/news/2019-04-01/behrouz-boochani-how-refugee-challenged-system-with-words/10799884 (accessed 21 July 2020).

Palmer, BC, Hafner, ML, & Sharp, MF (1994). *Developing Cultural Literacy through the Writing Process: Empowering All Learners*. Allyn & Bacon.

Rudd, K (2013). Transcript of broadcast on the regional resettlement arrangement between Australia and PNG. 19 July. Retrieved from https://pmtranscripts.pmc.gov.au/release/transcript-22762 (accessed 2 March 2021).

Savvas, M (2020). Life sentences—what creative writing by prisoners tells us about the inside. *The Conversation*, 20 February. Retrieved from https://theconversation.com/life-sentences-what-creative-writing-by-prisoners-tells-us-about-the-inside-130783.

Sparrow, J (2018). A place of punishment: *No Friend but the Mountains* by Behrouz Boochani: book review. *Sydney Review of Books*, 21 September. Retrieved from https://sydneyreviewofbooks.com/review/a-place-of-punishment-no-friend-but-the-mountains-by-behrouz-boochani (accessed 21 July 2020).

Torch (2020). In Prison. Retrieved from https://thetorch.org.au/what-we-do/in-prison.

Zable, A (2018). Australia's barbaric policy confronted by Boochani's prison memoir. *Sydney Morning Herald*, August 25. Retrieved from www.smh.com.au/national/australia-s-barbaric-policy-confronted-by-boochani-s-prison-memoir-20180821-p4zyt7.html (accessed 22 July 2020).

Zolkos, M. (2019). Registers of undesirability, poetics of detention: Jean Améry on the Jewish exile and Behrouz Boochani on the Manus Prison. In M. Zolkos, *Jean Améry*. Springer International Publishing, pp. 55–84.

5

CASTAWAYS

"That boy might be happy if he would stay at home, but if he goes abroad, he will be the most miserable wretch that was ever born" (Defoe, 1988 [1719], p.6) remarked Robinson Crusoe's mother at the beginning of Daniel Defoe's novel as Crusoe pined for adventure and experience on the oceans far away from his home. While the warning here from Crusoe's mother echoes through the rest of his 18th-century shipwreck tale, the statement acts as a stark caution to those other castaways who found themselves wrecked, especially during the same imperialist era of sea voyages and exploration. There is something to learn from the experience of the shipwrecked, the castaway and the isolated in the context of this book and the spectrum of how it has been written about, by the individual, both 'inside' the experience and after their return, and from interviews and fictional interpretations by others. Robinson's mother's warning isn't just one we can appreciate for the hopeful avoidance of tragedy and physical misery; it is a caveat for the emotional turmoil being castaway has left on many who followed in Robinson's footsteps. As McMahon writes, "it is the text of the accident that can instruct us as to the properties of textual meaning and its various makers: authors, cultures and ideologies" (McMahon, 2017, p.141). The writing of the 'wreck' and the castaway allows us to understand the writer and the text—to observe both their limits and the broader cultural and social impact of the writing while also understanding the seed that the event often plants in the castaway, that they can never fully relinquish control of the experience as they hope to revisit and recapture the ordeal for the rest of their lives.

This book focuses on writing and isolation, so as such, this chapter will focus on a selection of important examples from the era of exploration across the world's oceans, as this is when the traveller's journal, and writing of oceanic adventure and misfortune stories about castaways and disaster voyages for public consumption (and profit) became commonplace. The castaway is either a solitary person, or

DOI: 10.4324/9781003243267-5

group of people who are shipwrecked or stranded in an isolated location, often on an island. The history of successful sea faring in Southeast Asia goes back 50,000 years (Thompson, 2007) with Odysseus and St Paul early Western examples (McMahon, 2017), though it could be said that the history of unsuccessful sea voyages and their shipwrecks goes back even further.

The survival story of these people and the "activity of making do (working, improvising, addressing practical tasks) is important", writes Palmer (2016, p.xi), as it establishes how *Robinson Crusoe* was the first to popularly demonstrate the story of this "making do" in fiction, despite the many examples of explorers and journalists publishing diaries and pamphlets and writing non-fiction accounts prior to this. *Robinson Crusoe*'s success, accessibility and clear narrative structure enabled it to become the setting from which many other subsequent shipwreck and castaway tales were written in reference to, using the same "tripartite structure" (Thompson, 2007, p.5) of threat, disaster and aftermath to allow the castaway to reflect on and reconcile the event, while also providing a moral and dramatic structure for the reader to find escapism and a satisfying resolution within.

What can we ascertain from these castaways and the associated writing? Palmer posits that the most significant ideal to be drawn from the collective experiences and writing of the castaway is one of hope (Palmer, 2016), with a focus on how these people, marooned and suffering, kept going despite the utter hopelessness of their situations, not just to survive, to find food, build huts and to get rescued, but to also find inspiration and deeper meaning, to find the calmness to write a narrative about their experiences and to think beyond the minutia of their imprisonment with the optimism of finding closure and rescue.

Beyond the apparent optimism, however, when observing the castaway within the chapters of this book, and when looking at the literature of castaways, one of the prevalent themes that is also apparent is the tone of dissatisfaction that is attached to the writing of the experience. Many notable castaways have the romantic notion, often once they have been 'rescued', that their time in isolation is the richest of their lives, where they are the master of their domain in a way they had never and would never again experience, and where they can profit off their ordeal for the rest of their lives.

Romanticism of it all

One of the common elements when the writing of the isolated castaway, both for those whose experiences went comparatively well, and others who didn't fare so favourably, is the romanticism attached to the subsequent writing of the event. This is apparent with both participants and external authors. As Thompson writes, during the Romantic era of writers such as Keats, Byron, and Wordsworth in particular, there was an awareness that there was moral and existential influence from portraying oneself, or one's characters as suffering personas, whose misadventure was deemed romantic by readers and in turn lead to a "literary and cultural authority" (Thompson, 2007, p.273). As Keats wrote:

> I shall one day regret that I was not half drowned in Kirkudbright [sic] … [B]eing half drowned by falling from a precipice is a very romantic affair … being tumbled over a precipice into the sea—Oh it would make my fortune …
>
> *(Keats, 1958)*

This enthusiasm for misadventure allowed for commentary on the juxtaposition of the abandonment of the comforts of modern life alongside the deeper appreciation of the natural world—of the elements, of danger and of cultures unfamiliar to readers 'back home'. "To play the part of misadventurer was to play the part of someone who had been through a hugely revelatory, possibly even life-changing, test of character", writes Thompson (2007, p.273). When observing the trials of notable castaways and their fictional incarnations, there is evidence of the romantic persona and of one closer to nature, with a stronger moral and physical constitution, and an almost spiritual connection to their ordeal.

The romance of the castaway is also seen in the enthusiasm with which these experiences have been written and re-written about with the modern-day re-interpretation of the marooned survivor: with everything from the character played by Tom Hanks in the film *Castaway* (2000) through to the structure that a large variety of contemporary reality television programmes are aligned with, all focusing, ultimately, on the romance of the suffering, the survival and the ability to tell the story once returned. As Thompson writes, "Romantic readers would have absorbed many descriptions of shipwreck, famine, disease, fire, and other misfortunes that could befall a ship and its crew" (Thompson, 2007, p.61) and the shipwreck narrative itself became a subgenre of travel writing during the Romantic era.

There is another interesting echo in the writing of castaways and the influence it has had on tourism and the modern traveller and travel writer. It could be said that the experience of being castaway allowed these people (nearly always men) to travel away from their everyday existences and to 'find' themselves, and this is a trope that is often repeated in modern travel, as backpackers and 'off-the-beaten-path' travellers in pre-COVID years have invited the pain and discomfort of completing a two-week trek in Nepal, or an extended journey on a 3rd class sleeper train in India, "implicitly styling themselves as pilgrims" (Thompson, 2007, p.274) so as to gain greater insight into both themselves and the world through the experience of suffering through the unfamiliar.

The castaway tale has become a constant reminder of both human ambition and ingenuity, and of the harsh failings of the desire to master the ocean. These stories have also become important literary metaphors for the larger truths at play—of nationhood, human fallibility, and political and religious symbolism.

The islands these castaways have found themselves on have a significant role to play "as both literal and imaginary locations" according to McMahon (2017, p.19) which are important when considering the relationship between the geography of these 'far-off' places and the identity of the castaway during and after the experience. All these castaway tales begin on a beach in one manner or another and there is a change that takes place once the beach is crossed in the search for salvation and shelter. Renowned anthropologist Greg Dening takes this idea of the figurative significance of the landing site for many of these castaways further:

> Beaches are beginnings and endings. They are the frontiers and boundaries of islands. For some life forms the division between land and seas is not abrupt, but for human beings beaches divide the world between here and there, us and them, good and bad, familiar and strange.
>
> *(Dening, 1980, p.34)*

The most notable castaway tale that observed the 'beach crossing' in a manner that was both physically and narratively transformative was not the fictional Robinson Crusoe, but his real-life inspiration, Alexander Selkirk, who was marooned on the Juan Fernandez Archipelago 800km off the coast of Chile in the 18th century for 4 years and 4 months. He subsisted on crayfish and wild goats. Selkirk's story was written about by many journalists, playwrights, and novelists, though it was Daniel Defoe's adaptation of the tale into *Robinson Crusoe* that captured the public's attention.

Selkirk, Crusoe, and the original castaway story

Defoe's story of Robinson Crusoe was inspired by the true story of Alexander Selkirk, a Scottish sailor, born in 1680 in Fife, who was part of William Dampier's crew on a "booty-seeking voyage to South America" (Souahmi, 2001, p.23). Dampier wanted the gold nuggets the size of "hen's eggs" he had heard about in the Bolivian mines. Despite being 52 and past his prime, adventure had been in Dampier's veins for many years as he worked as a gunner in Sumatra, a logger in Mexico, a buccaneer, and a salvage merchant of Spanish galleons. This voyage promised to be no different. Dampier was also known for the travel writing of his adventures, where he offered his readers wild adventure, encounters with sharks, tornados, and pirates. He instructed his followers on the symptoms of scurvy and how to eat the tongue of a flamingo if you were in a tight spot.

The *St George* and the *Cinque Ports* departed England on 11 September 1703 bound for Madeira off the coast of Africa with Selkirk as the navigator of the *Cinque Ports*. They loaded up the holds with casks of wine and sailed down the Brazilian coast. The months passed at sea and scurvy and fever ripped through the crew. They became malnourished and ill, though they were not able to anchor and refit their ships until they encountered an island off the coast of Rio de Janeiro. They had been away for nearly six months and there was no treasure to show for it, only sickness and attempted mutinies. The ships rounded Cape Horn in foul weather and the crew expected to be wrecked on the rocks. Eventually the galleons limped into the island Más a Tierra (meaning 'closer to land' in Spanish) of the Juan Fernandez Archipelago off the Chilean coast. Dampier was lost and the crew were emaciated and discontent. Selkirk had got them there in February of

1704, though despite the *Cinque Ports*'s Captain Stradling's protests, Selkirk abandoned the ship to explore, leaving Stradling alone onboard only with the ship's monkey. Selkirk and the other crew paddled ashore to discover stands of sandal wood, crayfish in the bays and goats on the upper slopes. After replenishing their stores and health for a month they continued up the coast, plundering where opportunity arose, though there was dissatisfaction and infighting again as the booty was not shared evenly. In September that year they returned to Más a Tierra, with ship worms infested throughout the wood of the *Cinque Ports*. Captain Stradling did not want to linger, he wanted to enjoy the glory of their South American adventure back home. Selkirk refused to go, and instructed the crew to follow him, saying "in this ship none of them would go anywhere but to the ocean floor" (Souhami, 2001, p.78). Stradling and Selkirk fought, and Selkirk was accused of inciting a mutiny. Stradling eventually granted Selkirk's wish—he could stay on the island, and he could be food for the vultures for all he cared. And with that, Alexander Selkirk was marooned on Más a Tierra indefinitely.

During his 52 months on the island Selkirk found more peace than he would for the rest of his life. He had power and autonomy for the first time as he wandered along the cliffs and up the muddy inclines travelling across every inch of 'his' island. He made clothes from the skins of the abundant goats on the island, which were also one of his main food sources (and later of his lonely conquests). He tamed the feral cats left from previous voyages and set them to work killing the millions of rats, which had also jumped ship in years past. He was the "Monarch of all he surveyed" (Pratt, 1992) as his feet hardened like hooves. He read his only book, the Bible, while lying on the seal fur rugs in the rock shelter he built in a cradle of the hills above the main bay so he could see passing ships, he washed in streams and brushed his teeth with charcoal.

Interestingly, the writing of this castaway experience, the basis of the most famous castaway tale in modern history undoubtedly doesn't contain much, if any, input from Selkirk himself. The story became a battle between two rival seamen for notoriety post voyage.

After the mess of the Dampier expedition, a syndicate of councillors from Bristol pooled together the funds for a new, dual ship voyage with the *Duke* and *Duchess* built to head south to the Americas to plunder the riches the French and Spanish were profiting from. Woodes Rogers was to command the frigate *Duke*, a 320-tonne ship with 30 guns and double sheathed hulls to prevent the worms that had precipitated the Selkirk misadventure in the first place. Edward Cooke would be his second captain, and after seeing the fame and notoriety of French naval captain Jacques de Beacheane-Gouin's published diaries, they both kept journals of their own. Dampier, by this stage was nothing more than a figurehead on the voyage and his writing and adventure days were over.

The ships headed south in September 1708, plundering vessels in Tenerife, though with sailors succumbing to scurvy once again they pushed south towards the Americas and Cape Horn. By now there was also dysentery onboard as they approached the Falkland Islands (*Malvinas*). As January 1709 arrived Selkirk sat in his hut cooking the evening meal when two white-sailed ships came into view. Fearing that he would be left for another 4 years, Selkirk raced to the beach and dragged a burning log along the sand as a beacon. Yet with their confusion and caution, the men onboard the ships assumed the fire was a warning from an enemy, with Rogers writing in his journal: "We are all convinced the Light is on the shore, and design to make our Ships ready to engage, believing them to be French ships at anchor" (Rogers, 2019 [1712], p.149). They sent a small party ashore to investigate. The eight men arrived and saw a bedraggled castaway clothed in "Goat skins who look'd wilder than the first Owners of them" waving a white rag on a stick, he croaked "marooned", yet they initially thought he was some hybrid beast, "of a cannibal tribe" (Souhami, 2001, p.127). Selkirk gave them cooked food and fresh water, they saw the lobsters on the rocks, his hut, and domesticated goats. The men wrote of this encounter, "He had so much forgot his Language for want of Use, that we could scarce understand him, for he seem'd to speak his words by halves."

"Woodes Rogers called him the Governor of The Island and its Absolute Monarch. Selkirk could not explain that it was not like that. That the Island had governed him and was its own Monarch" (Souhami, 2001, p.129).

FIGURE 5.1 The statue of Alexander Selkirk on Isla Robinson Crusoe
Source: photograph by Ben Stubbs

FIGURE 5.2 The view that inspired Daniel Defoe and highlighted Selkirk's isolation for four years
Source: photograph by Ben Stubbs

Selkirk eventually spoke of his time on the island, taming goats, collecting wild plums from high mountain passes, the abundant fish, warm summers and of his near death fall down a precipice. Rogers saw a story in this. Selkirk had found a peacefulness and simplicity in his life that was absent before the experience. Now, as the men slaughtered the goats, salted hundreds of fish, killed seals for oil and chopped trees for storage, Selkirk was again faced with the melancholy "company of strategic thieves" (Souhami, 2001, p.133) as he had been accustomed to in his previous life.

Selkirk departed quietly as the ships receded from his home of 4 years and 4 months. He only took with him a handful of stones and his pet cat. The *Duke* and *Duchess* pillaged their way across the oceans eventually returning home in 1711, eight years since Alexander Selkirk had first left.

Captain Rogers had connected friends, including Richard Steele, the playwright, essayist and journalist, and Daniel Defoe, who wrote for the *Review*. Even with Rogers's literary connections, the other captain, Cooke, was the first to receive a book deal, detailing his adventures in *A Voyage to the South Sea and Round the World*. Notwithstanding his hope to centre the narrative on himself, the publisher advised that the book was to have the subtitle '*an Account of Mr Alexander Selkirk, his Manner of living and taming some wild Beasts during the four Years and four Months he liv'd upon the uninhabited Island of Juan Fernandes*'. Yet despite this imperative,

Selkirk's ordeal was confined to a solitary paragraph in his two-volume work, "Neither Rogers no Cooke had Dampier's skill for travel writing, his range, or flair for anecdote" writes Souhami (2001, p.163). Readers felt cheated and Cooke was prompted to release a second volume focusing on Selkirk's story. Cooke even interviewed Selkirk at the publisher's request this time, though he thought it dull to tell the story of a man alone on a 'Heap of Rocks', "We have a downright Sailor, whose only Study was how to support himself, during his Confinement and all his Conversations with Goats" (ibid., p.166).

Cooke detailed the moments they discovered this man running on the beach with a white flag. He itemised his tools and equipment and highlighted the location of his hut. Cooke wasn't interested in the psychology of his internment, the turmoil of his exile or of the prospect of re-telling his experience, as it was "irrelevant to the true purpose of the voyage" (Souhami, 2001, p.167), which was more about the heroism of Cooke himself.

Woodes Rogers, on the other hand, needed the funds from a successful book. He walked with a limp and had had half his face blown away from gunfire, his prospects were slim, and he wasn't getting any younger. The playwright Richard Steele met him in Coffee Houses in London and helped him fashion his book, *A Cruising Voyage Round the World* more closely around the story of Selkirk, which was also enhanced to make him seem a God-fearing Christian, a patriot, and the Governor of his Island. Facts were inconveniences as Rogers focused on the man, not the island in his adventure story of the castaway who moved from "piracy to piety" (Souhami, 2001, p.168) during his four years on the island. Rogers began by stating:

> Tho others, who give an Account of their Voyages, do generally attempt to imitate the Stile and Method which is us'd by Authors that write ashore, I rather chuse to keep to the Language of the Sea, which is more genuine, and natural for a Mariner.
>
> *(Rogers, 2019 [1712], p.50)*

As if to establish a sense of trust with his readers before he began to furnish the details of Selkirk's story, Rogers's 'journal' takes the reader through Brazilian islands, Paraguayan rivers and across Argentina before the crew finally arrive at Más a Tierra. At first, they feared the light they could see was from a Spanish garrison, though as they sent men ashore, the crew discovered the sailor from Fife who had been abandoned years before. Rogers detailed how trustworthy and noble Selkirk was, especially as he hid from the Spanish ship that came into the bay years before. He made notes of his equipment and how he "for the first eight months had much ado to bear up against Melancholy, and the Terror of being left alone in such a desolate place" (Rogers, 2019 [1712], p.151). Rogers quickly established how Selkirk managed to survive this ordeal however, writing that during his experience he, "employ'd himself in reading, singing Psalms, and praying; so that he said he was a better Christian while in his Solitude than ever he was before" (ibid., p151). Rogers concluded his 5 page section on Selkirk with more introspection and reflection than he drew on throughout the rest of his book, as he stated, "We may perceive by this Story the Truth of the Maxim, That Necessity is the Mother of Invention, since he found means to supply his Wants in a very natural manner, so as to maintain his Life" (ibid., p.154), also praising the simplicity and strength displayed by Selkirk after his rescue. Rogers, though, quickly reverted to form, stating that, "I must quit these Reflections, which are more proper for a Philosopher and Devine, than a Mariner and return to my own subject" (ibid., p.154).

Selkirk's own input into the writing of the experience aligned with Roger's account, though he was never compelled to write his own version before he died at only 41 years old in 1721. Perhaps after Richard Steele had also written his own version of Selkirk's ordeal, when he interviewed him extensively for the narrative, then forgot completely who Selkirk was when they ran into each other on the street just after publication, the narrative of him still being a castaway was finished. Selkirk did, however, continue to harbour ambitions to return to the island. The peacefulness, the identity he had there and the power in his isolation were not so apparent once he was back home.

What might be the most telling detail of Selkirk's experience is that despite him being more than comfortable financially after his years at sea, when Rogers had the idea of returning, and colonising the Juan Fernandez archipelago of which Más a Tierra was part, Selkirk was enamoured with the idea of re-living the best period of his life once again. Selkirk waited at the docks in Bristol for Rogers, drinking at the dive bars in hope that he could rekindle the event that defined him, though as months passed, the financing didn't eventuate and Selkirk disappeared, first to London, and then home to Scotland. Selkirk lived with his parents for a time, had a son and became addicted to alcohol. As Souhami writes, "He could not cope with its confinement and circumspection, the small-time conversation, the meals at table. He took no part in the daily round, was taciturn and at times in tears" (Souhami, 2001, p.184). He built a cave to live in at his home outside Fife in the south of Scotland, yet still he tried to integrate—buying land, orchards, and a large house. He married Sophia Bruce, though to him, she was only a distraction, the island was the only thing that resonated with him, and he disappeared once again to London.

Selkirk then worked as a naval officer, and it was during this period that the former acquaintance of Captain Woodes Rogers, the writer Daniel Defoe penned the very first English novel in 1719, titled *The Life and Strange Surprizing Adventures of Robinson Crusoe, of York, mariner: Who lived Eight and Twenty Year, all alone in an uninhabited Island on the Coast of America, near the Mouth of the Great River of Oronoque; Having been cast on Shore by Shipwreck, wherein all the Men perished but himself. An account of how he was at last as strangely deliver'd by Pyrates*, that was inspired by Selkirk's story.

The Robinson Crusoe/Alexander Selkirk tale also has a curious meta story to it and a personal relevance. Más a Tierra was re-named 'Robinson Crusoe Island' by the Chilean government in the 1960s in the hope of promoting greater tourism to the archipelago. The area is only accessible by infrequent container ship voyages or on a seven-seater plane from Santiago. In my career as a travel writer, I was inspired by the Crusoe/Selkirk story and the possibility of Selkirk's hut remaining on the island all these centuries later.

Selkirk did not have a wrecked ship to plunder for wood, building supplies and alcohol as his fictional inspiration did, so the most important part of Selkirk's stay was his lookout hut. Souhami writes that he would begin his watch "in the first light of the morning, at noon and at dusk. Behind the bay he climbed to his lookout, his vantage point. He scanned the encircling sea. He surveyed The Island, its tormented forms, its peaks and valleys" (Souhami, 2001, p.89).

Souhami observed that "the Island was a prison and he a mariner without a ship, a man without a voice" (ibid., p.3) and I was compelled to see what had happened to this shelter that had shaped so much of the subsequent narratives of Selkirk and Crusoe.

When I visited the island in 2009 for the *Sydney Morning Herald* my goal was to find the link, both physically and from a literary point of view between Selkirk's hut and the transition of this artefact as it is observed across a 300-year timeline. My host was local diver Pedro Niada who had lived on the island for more than a decade. He assured me that the remains of Selkirk's hut were well known to locals. Niada provided me with a map showing where the ruins of Selkirk's shelter were to be found, also underlining the ravines around Cerro Centinela, the site of Selkirk's lookout. "You have to think like a pirate", Pedro told me. "From here you can see all along the south and east coasts and if you were stranded here it would be the perfect spot to spot an incoming ship" (Stubbs, 2009). Over the course of a week on the island, I would walk across the mountains and wind-burned cliffs, I was alone, and my bag was packed with Niada's map, a water bottle, and a brown paper bag full of whatever the local bakery was selling that day—octopus empanadas one day, and cheese rolls the next. I would also carry copies of Souhami's book and Defoe's novel to help me understand the significance of the stories of this place when I would stop and read passages along the trail. I eventually discovered Selkirk's ultimately underwhelming hut, "Now just a collection of arranged stones, this was his sanctuary 300 years ago, where he constructed a sail tent, scrounged through the forest for turnips and watercress and supplemented his diet with goat, lobster and the occasional turtle" (ibid.) and it completed the full circle of my exploration, prompted by the search for the artifact of Selkirk's isolation that had continued to influence writers since the 18th century.

Writers re-telling the Crusoe tale

English romantic poet William Cowper first attempted to re-tell Selkirk's story through poetry, to try and access the emotions Selkirk might have felt in his poem *The Solitude of Alexander Selkirk*:

> I am monarch of all I survey,
> My right there is none to dispute,
> From the centre all round to the sea,

I am lord of the fowl and the brute.
O solitude! Where are the charms
That sages have seen in thy face?
Better dwell in the midst of alarms,
Than reign in this horrible place.
(Cowper, 1913, p.311)

Beyond the influence of Selkirk's story on Rogers, Cooke, Defoe and even my own subsequent writing as they relate directly to his experiences in Chile, there have also been more creative re-tellings of the exile experience inspired by Selkirk and Crusoe beyond the English-speaking world. Beyond the colonialist narrative of Defoe's in the 18th century, the re-purposing of the foundations of this story, in "an intensely self-aware textuality that complicates its own relationship to the *Robinson Crusoe* narrative from which it departs", Acquisto (2005, p. 346) writes of Saint-John Perse's 1904 poem *Images a Crusoe* where he focuses on seemingly minor objects from the novel to better highlight the impact of the exile experience on Crusoe the character. Whereas the Crusoe experience largely centres on the interactions between himself and Friday, and the overcoming of the odds that they are faced with (and to a large degree this is also what is captured in the brief writing of Selkirk's ordeal), Perse writes in second person, to forge a more intimate and vulnerable bond with the reader:

> You wept to remember the surf in the moonlight; the whistlings of the more distant shores; the strange music that is born and is muffled under the folded wing of the night, like the linked circles that are the waves of a conch, or the amplifications of the clamours under the sea.
>
> *(Translation by Acquisto, 2005, p.59)*

As Acquisto writes, this is full of poetic imagery, impactful syntax and intention, offering an "impulse" and emotion to the experience that is absent from previous renderings. This emotion also captures something of the repression of the longing we understand from Selkirk once he realised that he will never live as he did on 'his' island ever again. While the writing about Selkirk and Crusoe previously focused on the inventory of deeds the men achieved to ensure their survival, Perse centres the prose on the objects Crusoe had with him, allowing him to disappear through the symbolism of the scene and the emergence of his memories. In the subsequent poem *The City* Perse writes of Crusoe, back in England, closing his curtains to block out the sounds and smells of the city to better transport him back to 'his' island, something we could also imagine Selkirk doing in his cave back in Fife. This poem also expands on an important point that is detailed in many castaway narratives of both fiction and non-fiction, of the conflict between the "purity of the remembered island and the original 'truth'" (Acquisto, 2005, p.348) where the island was full of torment and struggle. It reminds us that the origins of the island experience as we have read them are subject to the inconsistencies of memory and the constant re-interpretation of the original experience.

The second example of creative re-telling of the Crusoe story comes from Elizabeth Bishop writing first person poetry which focuses on the memories Crusoe might have had, now living in England, long after the island has receded from his everyday existence. "Bishop's Crusoe is intent on looking back", states Acquisto (2005, p.351), and part of this looking back exposes the fragility of memory. Crusoe contends that all the previous re-tellings of his story were wrong, though he can't put his finger on the 'right' story, instead remembering Friday as a nice man who was his friend, and the haunting "Baa, baa, baa and shriek, shriek, shriek" (ibid., p.164) of the goats and gulls that were his companions. What these two versions show, along with the other re-purposing of Crusoe's story, such as Giraudoux's *Suzanne et la Pacifique* (1921), Tournier's *Vendredi ou les limbes du Pacifique* (1967) and Coetzee's *Foe* (1986), is that there are gaps that exist between these experiences of exile, from Selkirk, to Crusoe and beyond and these re-tellings, even in the modern era with the film *Castaway* (2000) or the reality television series *Alone* (2015–), demonstrate a complexity to the castaway experience that warrants continual re-casting across space, time and genre.

The stories of the *Wager*

One of the consistent themes with castaway writing is the lack of agency. In most cases the castaways themselves could not or did not want to write their own stories. In Europe in the early years of shipwreck narratives, castaways did not have either the education or motivation to write their stories, so the telling of these tales was often left to enterprising journalists and profit-seeking writers back home. Seeing the success of *Robinson Crusoe* and various published journals, it became commonplace for sailors to keep diaries in the hope of publishing their 'discoveries', which also served as a legacy to capture their accounts if they happened to be shipwrecked and castaway themselves.

When considering the tone of the castaway narrative, despite the proliferation of Romantic tales, it is important to remember that these stories often didn't have 'happy' endings, even if part of the crew managed to survive to tell their story. For some castaways, survival was the largest conclusion to reflect upon, when thousands of other explorers were drowning and disappearing each year on similar voyages (McMahon, 2017).

During the 18th century, further down the western coast of South America from Más a Tierra, there was another shipwreck which led to more castaway writing, though on this occasion it came from the shipwrecked sailors themselves.

In 1741 the British admiralty vessel, the HMS *Wager* with Captain David Cheap in charge was sent to South America's coastline to hamper the efforts of the Spanish to colonise and plunder. One of the 160 crew was John Byron, the poet's grandfather, and as they headed into Chilean Patagonia a hurricane smashed the ship between two rocks and forced them ashore on an unhospitable island. The men starved, died of exposure and hypothermia, and were killed both by their own companions and by the Indigenous Chilean Patagonians. Only 36 men made it home.

Reflecting perhaps what many of us have felt during the COVID-19 pandemic, the men from the *Wager* not only wrote about their angst, confusion, and misery, they acted it out. The men looted the wine casks and arms chests almost immediately upon their wrecking and "some men on the *Wager* became so paralytic that they drowned in the hold of the ship" (Hulme, 2011, p.140). Captain Cheap shot one of the drunk men in the head for insolence, and he took 2 weeks to die. This led to a fracture and the formation of two groups that decided on different paths home.

In all, four of the shipwrecked men wrote of their experiences, Captain David Cheap and three midshipmen, including John Byron, as well as numerous fictional accounts, such as Patrick O'Brian's *The Unknown Shore* (1959).

One group, led by gunner John Bulkeley, travelled via the Straits of Magellan around to Buenos Aires and eventually to England by 1743. The others, led by Cheap, went northwards. Interestingly, this is where the accounts of the conflicts, and their travails, help to sew a more complete story together.

As an interesting aside from the conflict that arose from the subsequent publishing that occurred after the *Wager*, the Admiralty instituted a rule in the aftermath "whereby all shipboard journals had to be turned over to the Admiralty at the end of the voyage" (Hulme, 2011, p.141) to maintain the reputation of the Navy and the Crown.

Byron wrote of the first encounter with the natives of the Patagonian islands that it gave them continual angst for what they might intend. As a group of Indians approached in canoes, he wrote, "It was evident, from their great surprise, and every part of their behaviour, as well as their not having one thing in their possession which could be derived from white people, that they had never seen such" (Byron, 2014 [1768], p. 28), yet Bulkeley wrote of this same encounter that the Indians were bowing and crossing themselves on arrival, and the other midshipman, Campbell insisted they wore ponchos and were "a good example to many well-educated Christians!" (Campbell, 1747, p.16).

They would later discover that the Spanish had a presence all around the area, including the major hub of Chiloé, when the Indians brought them mussels, three sheep and they bartered for two dogs, which the Englishmen promptly "roasted and eat [sic]" (Byron, 2014 [1768], p. 28), which was the first offence for their hosts. As Byron wrote, the second offence came when the Indians brought 50 or so women and children to live amongst them and help them, though the bereft and quarrelling men, "now subject to little or no control, endeavoured to seduce their wives, which gave the Indians such offence, that in a short time they found means to depart, taking everything along with them" (ibid., p.33).

The men split up due to their different approaches to find rescue, south with Bulkeley or north with Cheap. Bulkeley was mercenary in his approach, even throwing eight of his men overboard due to over-crowding, four were killed by Indians, and the other four were "bought and sold four different Times for a Pair of Spurs, a Brass Pan, Ostriches Feathers, and such like Trifles" according to Bulkeley's own published account (Bulkeley & Cummins, 1927 [1743], p.190).

There were obvious similarities and key differences in the writing of this shipwreck, whereby the men published accounts to make their allegiances key, to either condemn or support the actions of Captain Cheap, and, as with those who wrote Selkirk's story, to profit on the notoriety of their misadventure. The real depth in the analyses, reflections and the lasting impact comes from Byron's writing of the shipwreck experience though, which was not published until well after they had returned.

As Hulme writes of Byron's narrative from the shipwreck, "Only those who survive abjection write about it, and to write about one's own abjection involves finding a scene of redemption, the moment when things begin to look up" (Hulme, 2011, p.147). Byron was part of the crew that went northwards, and he portrayed the ordeal and its harshness to his readers in a manner that was unusual in tone compared to these normally moral and redemptive tales. Unlike the rashness of both Bulkeley and Cheap, Byron was more patient. He built himself a hut in the icy cold of their shipwrecked island and waited until he was forced to choose a direction to leave for, whereby he went with the expectations of Navy hierarchy and followed the Captain. Byron also saw more of the place he was inhabiting, much like Selkirk, and he was not solely focused on his own 'right' to find salvation as an English explorer. He noticed the mummified bodies in the burial places of the Kawéskar and Chono Indians, the manner in which women dived for sea-eggs and how shelters and canoes were built in this place they literally crashed into.

Byron begs, on hands and knees, for salvation from the Indigenous people and two women in their wigwam gave him warmth, allowing him to sit by the fire and a fish to eat, despite it being their last food. His "patronesses" gave him a blanket and went out into the night to fish for more food. They were the wife and daughter of the cacique, local leader, and on his return the women are beaten "half to death" for their display of compassion.

This flipped the conventional colonial encounter of the era, the white men of the *Wager* saw themselves and the hopelessness of their situation in the way the Indigenous women were brutalised by the men, who "exercise a most despotic authority over their wives, whom they consider in the same view they do any other part of their property, and dispose of them accordingly" writes Hulme (2011, p.148). A Chono man, Martín, arrived with authority from the Spanish on Chiloé and he agreed to guide the group northwards in exchange for their salvaged barge.

Byron wrote about his experience of shipwrecked isolation long after it had faded from public interest; the psychological impact being the main reason that compelled him to do so, "his whole worldview was also undermined on that Patagonian shore: an experience which must have destroyed his understanding of his place in the scale of human superiority" (Hulme, 2011, p.149). The trauma of the event could only be written about, and reflected on, once it was not the "climax" of his own personal story, a clear distinction from the Selkirk tale. In 1768 Byron had become a Commodore and had circumnavigated the world. Byron's writing of this experience allowed him to re-establish the order in the world he existed in once again, "when status and hierarchy have been restored and made permanent, and when it is the Patagonians who are abject, not the Englishman" (ibid., p.151). This event also rippled throughout his own family, as his grandson, to become the poet Lord Byron, would write his own expression of the *Wager* disaster in *Don Juan* (Thompson, 2007).

Australian castaways and Indigenous encounters

Being an Australian during lockdown, I'm quite naturally drawn to the stories of shipwrecks and isolation across the largest island in the world, with 3000 shipwrecks recorded by the Australian National Shipwreck Database between 1788 and 1901 and more than 8000 in total (DEWHA, 2008).

In Australia during colonisation, the main sea-faring narratives centred on the 'discovery' and invasion of the continent from many explorers similar in statue and world view to the Dampier-esque sailors of the earlier shipwreck narratives. The tone of the Australian castaway narratives was markedly different to their European Romantic contemporaries however, being graphic more than melancholic, and vivid in the specific detail with the aim of instilling fear and humility in the reader (McMahon, 2017) rather than showing endorsement for Providential design and redemption. This is most prominently seen in the re-telling of the 1629 *Batavia* wreck, when 125 people were subsequently murdered off the Albrolhos Islands in Western Australia. This story has been re-cast in theatre, fiction, script, and poetry many times. This fearful tone was also evident in the poetry of the *Cataraqui* wreck off King Island when 400 people died in 1845, as seen with Samuel Prout Hill's poem published months after the event:

> Though his children are weeping—they scarce know for why;
> His faith is unshaken, and death he can dare;
> But 'tis horror to watch his young budding hopes die.
> Yet louder still louder the storm rolls around—
> All frantic and madly the shup rushes by—
> When hark! God of mercy! That terrible sound,
> The storm stands abash'd, so piteous the cry.
> Then shriek upon shriek rent apart the wild air
> The mother and child, oh! How fondly they clung;
> And above the rude wind might be heard the faint prayer
> The death-speaking wail of both aged and young.
>
> *(Hill, 1845, p.4)*

In Australia during this era there were many cases of castaways ending up within Indigenous communities of Northern Australia when broader integration was far from common, "Europeans who lived with Indigenous people, often regarded by the wider colonial society and sometimes by themselves as 'captives', look more like refugees" (Maynard & Haskins, 2018).

James Murrells was an English sailor who was aboard the *Peruvian* in 1846 transporting hardwood from Sydney to China when they struck an unseen reef on the Minerva Shoal out from New Caledonia. The book written about his shipwreck experience by Edmund Gregory was the breathlessly titled *The Narrative of JAMES MURRELLS' ("JEMMY MORRILL") Seventeen years exile among the wild blacks of North Queensland, and his life and shipwreck and terrible adventures among savage tribes; their manners, customs, languages, and superstitions; also Murrells rescue and return to civilization*. While unashamedly racist, as was common for the place and the era, the book details the author's interviews with Murrells before he died. Of the 21 who survived the initial wreck of the *Peruvian* and boarded a raft, only seven survived the 42 days drifting on the ocean:

> We had more hooks but no more line. There were plenty of sharks about, some of which we tried to catch. The captain devised a plan to snare them with a running bowline knot, which we managed as follows: we cut off a leg of one of the men who died, lashed it at the end of an oar for a bait, and on the end of another oar we set the snare, so that the fish must go through the snare to get at the bait. Presently one came, which we fortunately captured and killed with the carpenter's axe. We cut his head off and flayed him. The sailmaker's hunger was greater than his caution, for. while he held its head in his hands eating it, he incautiously put his hand in its mouth, the jaws closed, which gave him a severe bite—. so much so that it stayed his hunger for a time.
>
> *(Gregory, 1896, p.14)*

The party finally arrived at the beach of Cape Cleveland, now modern Townsville. After weeks of subsistence camping, and with only four of the group still alive, the Indigenous Birri-Gubba people made contact (McCalman, 2014). The party was separated eventually, and Gregory wrote of Murrells's curiosity at the smoking ceremonies, corroborees, and familial relationships as they were brought inside the community at their shipwreck location. It is not quite written in a romantic tone, though it is far from the narrative of encounters with 'savages' that is seen in much Anglo-Saxon accounts of first encounters with Indigenous peoples in the same era. Murrells told Gregory in interviews how they learned to forage for roots and nuts, to understand the language and to hunt, "We spent our time wandering about with them on their fishing excursions, and in learning how to snare ducks, wild turkeys, and other bush birds" (Gregory, 1896, p.21) as he estimated they had been living together for 5–6 months.

The narrative explored how Murrells stayed, year after year, long after his other 3 ship mates had died. He learned more than he realised of the place he lived and, while still clearly hoping for 'rescue' back to the white communities of his past, there is a patience to his existence, of foraging for honey and bread fruit, of observing tribal conflicts and interactions and using Indigenous place names when describing exchanges. There is an obvious connection with his hosts, when he remarked of the way the Indigenous were treated by the callous white settlers as "a sad reward for all their kindness to us" (Gregory, 1896, p.27).

Eventually, though, as white settlers encroached further and further into the Indigenous nations of Northern Australia, Murrells revealed himself at a cattle station and it was only then that he realised that it was 1863, and he had been 'marooned' for 17 years. Intriguingly, when the settlers tried give him dry damper he resisted as he had been with a hunting party that had a full cache of wallabies, and he wasn't hungry; he couldn't stomach the black tea for the foreign taste of sugar and he resisted putting clothes on as he wanted to return to the tribe to inform them of what is going on before he abandoned his castaway life.

> They asked me if I would come back in a few days. I told them no, I should probably be away three or four moons. They then said "you will forget us altogether" and when I said good-bye, the man I was living with burst into tears, so did his gin [sic], and several other gins [sic] and men. It was a wild touching scene. The remembrance of all their past kindnesses came up powerfully before, and quite overpowered, me.
>
> *(Gregory, 1896, p.30)*

The final thought Murrells has as he left his companions who had cared for him and included him in their lives for 17 years is one of conflict. He thinks that he wants a 'civilised' life, though it is tinged with melancholy, as the old way he lived his life "may better be imagined than described" (ibid., p.31) he realised as a parting thought. In 1863, soon after he joined the British community, he published a pamphlet describing his time, and affection for the Birri-Gubba as a response to the many questions and prompts he received about his time with them, which helped "to create a dignified, reasonable persona through which he could make a plea on behalf of the Aboriginal people of the region that might be heard by readers" (Dortins, 2018, p.49).

Gregory released a second edition of this book shortly after Murrells died in 1865, where he bumped him aside as author (Dortins, 2018), and tellingly Gregory removed his "closing plea on behalf of the Birri-gubba and their neighbours for reciprocal good treatment and for a division of land" (ibid., p.51).

Gregory also wrote that he wished he had pushed Murrells for more detail on the adjustment and the internal struggle, rather than just focusing on the 'mere fringe' of the experience:

> This edition is published with the author's belief that the remarkable narrative will be quite as interesting to the new generation as to the old. The first edition of this work was written partly to satisfy an urgent public demand, and partly to provide funds for Murrells' immediate necessities.
>
> *(Gregory, 1896, p.5)*

Reflecting the dissatisfaction that many castaways seemed to have post-experience, *The Argus* of 18 May 1863 wrote that Murrells had a "taint" about him and his inability to let go of his experience for the rest of his short life.

There were many castaway stories in early colonisation in Australia which demonstrated a connection to the land, to the Indigenous people and of the deeper relationship than was appreciated by most white settlers at the time.

Narcisse Pelletier was only 14 when he boarded the *Saint-Paul* in Marseille for a voyage to India as a cabin boy with a cargo of Bordeaux wine (Macklin, 2019). On the return trip, they picked up 300 Chinese miners bound for Australia's gold rush, though when they struck a reef off New Guinea, the miners were deposited on Rossel Island and the crew rowed their longboat 1200km across the Coral Sea to Cape York, the northernmost tip of Australia (Anderson, 2009). After 12 days at sea, Pelletier was close to death, so he was abandoned near Cape Direction. The Sandbeach People, or Uutaalnganu, took him in and cared for him. He lived with them and developed into a man with his Indigenous carers, living with them for 17 years until, "In early April 1875, a trepang fishing brig anchored off Night Island and its sailors 'rescued' at gunpoint a naked, spear-carrying white man with chest scarifications and an elongated earlobe" (McCalman, 2014).

The rhythm, language, and culture of 19th-century France was completely foreign to Pelletier when he returned, and he had extreme difficulty with the readjustment. "Locals believed he'd succumbed to primitive nostalgia for the life and people of the Sandbeach," writes McCalman (2014).

In 1876 French savant and former surgeon Constant Merland interviewed Pelletier and told his story in the book *Dix-sept ans chez les sauvages: Les adventures de Narcisse Pelletier* to re-tell the tale, while also providing Pelletier with some income as he readjusted. Whether Pelletier ever received any payment is still a point of contention (Macklin, 2019).

To demonstrate the disconnect between language and culture with the re-telling of the castaway story, author Stephanie Anderson noted in her book *Pelletier: The Forgotten Castaway of Cape York* that what happened to Pelletier once he returned to France "is not known in Australia" (Anderson, 2009, p.14), and conversely, there are large gaps in the original French re-telling around Indigenous tribes, locations, and events. This prompted Anderson to intervene, by translating the original French version of Merland's narrative, accompanied by her own Australian research of the ethnographic accounts of the Cape York region in the 19th century and an attached appendix from a local ethnographer, Athol Chase, who lived in the same Cape York region for 30 years. She re-tells this story to take advantage of the greater awareness offered by various versions of the story while also attempting to "make Merland's text as ethnographically and ethnohistorically useful as possible" (ibid., p.14). Anderson also modernises the tone and Merland's "condescending attitudes to non-European people" (ibid., p.23), indeed, the word 'savages' in the title is evidence of this. Where possible, Anderson also notes that in this re-telling of the castaway narrative she tries to include as many published accounts as possible from the Indigenous people themselves, though the examples are sparse.

Beyond the romanticism, Anderson highlights how multiple accounts of shipwreck experiences are important across a variety of genres, especially if there is enforced or voluntary separation, to better understand the tone of the experience and its eventual reception. In the *Peruvian*'s Captain Pinard's account, there are many differences to Pelletier's recollection, as told to Merland, such as how many were on the Coral Sea longboat, what the Chinese miners were told as they were left on the remote and waterless atoll and why Pelletier was eventually stranded—the captain insisting that he missed a roll call, whereas Pelletier contended that he was gathering water with the crew and got abandoned by the tide. Either way, the resulting 17 years marooned and living with the Uutaalnganu was the consequence.

Anderson contends that despite Merland's account and the various pieces of journalism in Australia and France about Pelletier's experience, there was (and will continue to be) a gap in the intercultural understanding of his period as a castaway with the Uutaalnganu, as no one sought to interview him in-depth, not just about the external happenings of day-to-day life, but of the immense emotional and social adjustment that he underwent in his early years on Cape York.

What does remain in written form that expands the written evidence of Pelletier's isolation is a series of songs and letters written by Pelletier from his time marooned in Cape York. He only wrote three letters after his 'rescue' and all are

FIGURE 5.3 Narcisse Pelletier
Source: reproduced with permission from State Library of Queensland

perfunctory at best, detailing the basics of his overall encounter to his parents, his sore leg and that he is reluctantly onboard a ship returning to France. The other textual inclusions are more unique, if extremely culturally questionable. Pelletier recalled the music of the Uutaalnganu during his time with them, and poet and composer Edouard Garnier arranged his recollections into a musical score so there would be a lasting record of this unique angle of his time. This ethnomusicology is raw, and the manner in how this 'music' was elicited is dubious according to Macklin as he "made an ambitious attempt to have Narcisse perform the chants and songs of the Night Island clan as he transcribed the 'melodies; and 'lyrics' into the Western system of staff notation" (Macklin, 2019, p.288) unfortunately without input from the Uutaalnganu. Despite this, it remains one of the most vivid and unembroidered recollections of Pelletier's time in Cape York.

A female castaway perspective

Within this exploration of the Australian castaway (and of nearly all castaway stories for that matter) there is a conspicuous absence of female stories. Part of this is due to the era and the social barriers imposed on women to remain 'home' and 'safe' while the men explored and conquered. One fascinating deviation from this is the story of Barbara Thompson. She was a Scottish woman who migrated to Australia at 16 and eloped with her sailor husband William Thompson to Moreton Bay from Sydney. The couple headed to Cape York in 1844 on a salvage mission for whale oil off a wreck they had identified, though bad weather capsized their own ship in the process, with her husband and the rest of the crew drowning. Thompson was rescued by the Kaurareg people on Mulalag Island and she lived with them for five years until the 16th of October 1849 when the scientific ship *Rattlesnake* came into view of their isolated beach. When she was discovered, young naturalist Oswald Brierly wrote in his journal that she initially had the manner "of a person just waking up from a deep sleep and had not had time to collect her ideas" (Moore, 1979, p.77). The ship stayed moored off the beach for many weeks, and Thompson, who by now spoke "a combination of working-class Scottish English and Kaurareg language" (Dortins, 2018) told her story to Brierly. Brierly was open and curious, with no ulterior motive in his listening. As McCalman writes, "Brierly's fascination with Indigenous people and culture went well beyond the standard Enlightenment vogue for collecting taxonomies and artefacts" (McCalman, 2013, p.109). He admired them and was proud to call many his friends from his travels around Australia.

Brierly was given the name *Tarrka*, alongside Thompson's *Giom* as she had been known, as they remained offshore. In this safe space Thompson told Brierly of the cultural differences and humour evident in her experience and Brierly would write in his journal that he would spend entire days "engaged in getting words and making notes of Mrs Thompson's information" (Moore, 1979, p.83). Brierly's past fascination with both sketching different people he met, and of learning the Indigenous languages he encountered allowed him to instil a sense of authenticity in the account he wrote of

Thompson's castaway story, for which she (being illiterate) was not able to write. Brierly however credited her inability to write with her vivid memory for the details of her life that was "remarkably observing" (McCalman, 2013, p.113) providing an intimate account of her time with the Kaurareg while also assisting him "getting words and sentences in the *ngyaoommie Kowrariga* [Kaurareg language]" (Moore, 1979, p.89). Thompson would tell Brierly of the social relations of the women in the community, of their modes of childbirth, weaving, finding medicines, and the many norms and taboos of her adopted home. She told him of their trading and hut building, of the symbolism of death and ritual initiations and warfare demonstrating a cultural depth that had not been seen in the writing of Aboriginal Australia by outsiders before this. As she became more fluent, and more comfortable, she "poured out stories illustrating the love and care showered on her by adoptive relatives and friends" (McCalman, 2013, p.115), even telling the story of an encounter with another tribe that had another castaway with them, of Malay or Portuguese origin, yet when she was offered to marry this castaway because of their similar stories, she chose to stay on Muralag Island with the Kaurareg.

A notable difference in the writing of Thompson's story was with the tone and intention of Brierly:

> There was no haste to make public an account of her experiences. Brierly's notes were not made with a view to publication, and it seems he never sought to bind this record of her story into the corset of an orderly narrative.
>
> *(Dortins, 2018)*

Another key difference in this account was the gradual nature of the separation, showing the strong notion of 'two lives' seen with many castaways. The *Rattlesnake* stayed for 9 weeks, and the women would bring frequent gifts of turtle eggs, baskets, and yams to *Giom*. Brierly would write of the affection Thompson was afforded by the Kaurareg, and as they prepared to depart, they paddled canoes to the edge of the ship:

> A very old woman who called herself her mother came with them crying and showing a shell which she wore round her neck, saying it was one the white woman had left in her bag on the island and that she kept it in remembrance of her.
>
> *(Moore, 1979, p.231)*

The ship eventually departed back to Sydney in February 1850 and the *Sydney Morning Herald* and the *Brisbane Courier* published brief "sanitised" (McCalman, 2013, p.122) accounts of her castaway period, though the lack of conflict or sexual tension according to McCalman saw Thompson's story fade from public knowledge, especially seeing as Brierly's own journals of the experience remained unpublished in his lifetime. After 'rescue' Thompson found her parents still alive in Sydney. She married multiple times and died in 1912.

Contemporary castaways

The romanticism of the castaway and the writing of the experience is not something that has been confined to the imperialist era of exploration either. There have been many modern reincarnations of this trope in fiction, such as the film *Castaway* (2000) and Yann Martel's *The Life of Pi* (2001). It is interesting that the north of Australia has also been the location for a modern castaway as it was for Pelletier, Thompson, and Murrells.

In 1987 David Glasheen was the chairman of a publicly listed gold and platinum exploration company. He had $10 million in shares and a property portfolio. When the stock market crashed, he tried to maintain his highflying life for four years, before finally his debts caught up with him and his marriage ended.

The familiar tropes are mentioned at the beginning of this modern incarnation of the *Crusoe* tale, of it being "wild, eccentric, romantic and sad" (Glasheen, 2019, p.i) of his decision to cast himself away in the Coral Sea in *The Millionaire Castaway*.

With a new girlfriend and failing health, Glasheen saw escape as his only option. "Why don't we pack it all in and go and live on a deserted island?", he wondered (Glasheen, 2019, p.35). An enterprising friend located Restoration Island off the coast of Lockhart River, the northernmost community on East Coast Australia. The traditional owners are the Kuuku Ya'u people.

Initially all Glasheen saw was the romance of his self-imposed castaway island. The first descriptions he wrote were full of promise: "I felt weirdly overcome with emotion. I had been so excited to finally see the place, and it had exceeded my expectations" (Glasheen, 2019, p.43). Glasheen saw white beaches, palm trees and possibility. The romance of the Crusoe ideal filled his head, until he looked closer. The site was full of rubbish, a derelict caravan, smashed windows and evidence of the greed of the caretaker to offload the island to this idealist. Glasheen ventured to the top of the island and the view of the Coral Sea is enough to convince him to stay. The romance of 'owning' an island propelled him through years of financing, partnerships and development plans on this island that is 30 kilometres north of where Pelletier ended up.

Glasheen portrayed himself as a simple man, where his reception of a more primitive way of life has meaning and value, especially considering that he 'chose' this life, instead of his shipwrecked forebears. As Hayden White writes, this primitive notion "simply invites men to be themselves, to give vent to their original, natural, but subsequently repressed desires; to throw off the restraints of civilisation and thereby enter into a kingdom that is *naturally* theirs" (White, 1972, p.26). This shedding of restraints, of perceived belonging of what is 'theirs' is evident in Glasheen's writing of his island experience. Less cynically, it is also evident in the way Selkirk, Pelletier and Murrells all reacted to their reintegration into their old lives, as if this immersion into a world where they could act out their repressed desires and natural inclinations created a friction in their world view from which they were unable to fully recover from. As Anderson writes of this castaway ideal, "they left behind one set of social and cultural rules, but could only survive by learning another" (Anderson, 2009, p.25).

Glasheen's experience only moved away from the conquering and 'ownership' mindset of his predecessors when he realised his position, both physically and culturally. He learned of the gap in living conditions for the local Indigenous people, their mistreatment in this area despite being the traditional owners and the need to consult them of his plans, thus alerting him that his dreams of paradise in the 21st century are necessarily more complicated.

Eventually he became the caretaker of the island. He cultivated vegetables, cleaned up the generations of rubbish left there, welcomed visitors, and built a shack on the island. The stubbornness is curious in this context. He arrived with an image of what being marooned would be and all else seems pushed aside in pursuit of this image. The fundamental element of castaways in an historical sense is the notion of choice. While many of them would have chosen to stay once they realised the freedom and peace it afforded them, none had chosen to be marooned in the first place. This modern affectation is also something replicated in reality television, with Bear Grylls-style programs such as *Alone* enlisting survival 'experts' to outlast one another in situations the shipwrecked found themselves in only a few hundred years before.

In the epilogue of Glasheen's memoir, after a violent storm forced him off the island, he reflected on the injustice shown to the Indigenous people and how he hoped he could stay and care for their land in the future. He realised, like Selkirk, that this castaway experience had become the centre of his entire life, "The grass could—literally—not be any greener anywhere else on Earth, and I'd give my last breath fighting to stay on this piece of land" (Glasheen, 2019, p.317). The book ends with Glasheen's reflections on mortality. He wrote about Robinson Crusoe and of Masafumi Nagasaki, the Japanese man who marooned himself on a tropic island in southern Japan until authorities removed him at the age of 82 into aged care.

It raises the interesting question of what happens to the self-styled castaway in the 21st century? Just as Pelletier couldn't adjust to rural France after he was rescued, and Selkirk lived the rest of his short life in dissatisfaction and at the bottom of a bottle, Glasheen's story doesn't seem like it will have the happy ending he initially envisaged either when he eventually has to be 'rescued' himself.

What this latest castaway contribution also demonstrates, however, is that the universal themes within all castaway writing, evident since the Egyptian *Tale of the Shipwrecked Sailor*, of transformation and renewal, are still central in the 21st century.

References

Acquisto, J (2005). The Lyric of Narrative: Exile, Poetry, and Story in Saint-John Perse and Elizabeth Bishop. *Orbis Litterarum*, 60(5), 344–356.

Anderson, S (2009). *Pelletier: The Forgotten Castaway of Cape York*. Melbourne Books.

Bulkeley, J & Cummins, J (1927 [1743]). *A Voyage to the South Seas in His Majesty's Ship the Wager in the Years 1740–1741*. George G. Harrap & Co.

Byron, J (2014 [1768]). *The Narrative of the Honourable John Byron Containing an Account of the Great Distresses Suffered by Himself and His Companions on the coast of Patagonia from the Year 1740, till Their Arrival in England 1746: With a Description of St. Jago de Chili, and the Manners and Customs of the Inhabitants, also a Relation of the Lofs of the Wager Man of War, One of Admiral Anson's Squadron*. S. Baker et al.

Campbell, A (1747). *The sequel to Bulkeley and Cummins's voyage to the South-seas*. S Powell.

Cowper, W (1913). *The Complete Poetical Works of William Cowper*. Oxford University Press.

Defoe, D (1988 [1719]) *Robinson Crusoe*. Aerie Books.

Dening, G (1980). *Islands and Beaches: Discourse on a Silent Land: Marquesas 1774–1880*. Dorsey Press.

DEWHA (2008). National shipwreck database. Australian Ocean Data Network dataset. Retrieved from https://catalogue.aodn.org.au:443/geonetwork/srv/en/metadata.show?uuid=516811d7-cb5f-207a-e0440003ba8c79dd.

Dortins, E (2018). *The Lives of Stories: Three Aboriginal-Settler Friendships*. ANU Press.

Glasheen, D (2019). *The Millionaire Castaway: The Incredible Story of How I Lost My Fortune but Found New Riches Living on a Deserted Island*. Affirm Press.

Gregory, E (1896). *Narrative of James Murrells' ("Jemmy Morrill") Seventeen Years Exile Among the Wild Blacks of North Queensland, and his Life and Shipwreck and Terrible Adventures Among Savage Tribes; Their Manners, Customs, Languages and Superstitions; Also Murrells Rescue and Return to Civilization*. Archive Digital Books Australia.

Hill, S (1845). The Cataraqui. *Colonial Times and Tasmanian* (26 December), 4.

Hulme, P (2011). Abject in Patagonia: stories from the Wager. *Studies in Travel Writing*, 15 (2), 135–156.

Keats, J (1958). *The Letters of John Keats*, 2 vols (ed. HE Rollins). Harvard University Press).

Macklin, R (2019). *Castaway: The Extraordinary Survival Story of Narcisse Pelletier, a Young French Cabin Boy Shipwrecked on Cape York in 1858*. Hachette Australia.

Maynard, J & Haskins, V (2018). Living with the locals: Six extraordinary first contact stories of friendship and survival. *ABC RN*, 6 April. Retrieved from www.abc.net.au/news/2018-04-06/living-with-the-locals-stories-of-first-contact-survival/9613098.

McCalman, I (2013). *The Reef: A Passionate History*. Penguin Books.

McCalman, I (2014). Shipwrecked and kidnapped: a tale of two castaways on the Great Barrier Reef. *ABC RN*, 25 July. Retrieved from www.abc.net.au/radionational/programs/archived/hindsight/shipwrecked-and-kidnapped:-a-tale-of-two-castaways/5623562.

McMahon, E (2017). Accidents of empire: Shipwrecks and castaways. In *Islands, Identity and the Literary Imagination*. Anthem Press, pp. 133–176.

Moore, D (1979). *Islanders and Aborigines at Cape York: An Ethnographic Reconstruction Based on the 1848–1850 'Rattlesnake' Journals of O.W. Brierly and Information He Obtained from Barbara Thompson*. Humanities Press.

Palmer, C (2016). *Castaway Tales: From Robinson Crusoe to Life of Pi*. Wesleyan University Press.

Pratt, M-L (1992) *Imperial Eyes: Travel Writing and Transculturation*. Routledge.

Rogers, W (2019 [1712]). *A Cruising Voyage Around the World*. Good Press.

Souhami, D. (2001). *Selkirk's Island: The Original Robinson Crusoe*. Orion Books.

Stubbs, B. (2009). By name, by nature. *Sydney Morning Herald*. Retrieved from www.traveller.com.au/by-name-by-nature-iefh (accessed 24 January 2021).

Thompson, C (2007). *The Suffering Traveller and the Romantic Imagination*. Oxford University Press.

White, H (1972). The forms of wildness: Archaeology of an idea. In E Dudley & M Novak (eds), *The Wildman Within: An Image in Western Thought from the Renaissance to Romanticism*. University of Pittsburgh Press, pp. 3–37.

6

WRITING, ISOLATION, AND WAR

In the context of this book focusing on writing and confinement it is valuable to look at the writing from within war and conflict which offers a 'from below' perspective. This chapter will concentrate on a selection of mainly Western assessments written by those who were confined and isolated within the eye of battle and conflict in the two world wars, whether this be in the trenches of the Somme, in an annexe in Amsterdam or administering morphine in a Belgian field hospital. There is a wealth of writing 'about' war, though as this book focuses specifically on isolation and confinement, I will look only at those examples which demonstrate the intimate nature of the experience, often as a form of travel writing itself, of the strange and unfamiliar places those impacted by war and conflict would find themselves.

Trench writing and the First World War

The symbolism of the trench within the First World War became so prevalent that the notion of writing from 'within' became somewhat obscured in the process. There became a difference, however, in the two stages of existence in war: life outside the trench, and life from within the trench. They became "two distinguishable worlds" (Fussell, 1975, p.41): one of zig-zagging passages with duck boards to walk on, walls of sandbags, sticks and corrugated iron six to eight feet deep and tangles of barbed wire above where they couldn't raise their heads above the lip for fear of being picked off by a sniper; and the other of reading newspaper reports and official accounts of the war effort away from the pressure of battle. By the time of the Great War, it was common for soldiers to not only be literate, but to have clear literary tendencies as they waited in the mud of the trenches for battle. These soldiers were writing of the war on their own terms—ordinary people from within the gutters of conflict. This was something revolutionary when compared to earlier battles and the perspectives that only came from the higher ranks and official historians (Fussell, 1975).

DOI: 10.4324/9781003243267-6

This form of writing could also be seen as an early contributor to the 'from below' historiographical practice. As the re-thinking of history broadened in the 1960s and 70s with Barthes and later Hayden White's *Metahistory: The Historical Imagination in Nineteenth-Century Europe* (1973) the emergence of on-the-ground and immersed point of views provided an alternative interpretation of the past. This 'from below' approach has been successfully used by scholars Robert Darnton and Carlo Ginzburg, in *The Cheese and the Worms: The Cosmos of a Sixteenth-Century Miller* (1980) and *The Great Cat Massacre: And Other Episodes in French Cultural History* (1984) respectively, as they utilised the perspectives of 'ordinary' people as a counterpoint to official sources to comment on the differences between 'high' and 'low' perspectives within history. The written accounts of soldiers, nurses and journalists within the trenches, field hospitals and staging areas of battle is a clear early example of this alternate view of the official histories of war.

During the First World War it is noted that the length of trenches, on the Allied side alone, measured nearly 20,000 kilometres, so it is little wonder that the men would find both the time and the impulse to write while confined in this labyrinth, often marked with the street names of London—Piccadilly, Regent, Strand—as a tongue-in-cheek attempt at gentrification. The German trench 'streets' were labelled 'Bitter' and 'Beer', 'Ale' and 'Pilsen' by the soldiers as a morbid parody of a real city, when in reality they were "wet, cold, smelly and thoroughly squalid" (Fussell, 1975, p.46). Indeed, there were even national styles of the trenches: the German trenches were clean, comfortable, and precise often with bunk beds, mirrors and water tanks; the British trenches, seeing as they assumed they would be impermanent structures, were ramshackle, shabby and muddy; and in the French ditches, soldiers recalled smelling wonderful cooking wafting from within (ibid., p.48). It is from inside these spaces of war that some of the most interesting writing from the period emerged.

From within the trenches the first writing that occurred was the nightly casualty reports to be sent out of the trench along with the letters of condolence. Coming from the men inside, it was mainly journals and letters home that were written to the outside world, though they also wrote of the experience of 'being' in the ditch. Poet Louis Simpson wrote of being in the trench when shelling began, of lying face down in the mud and crawling into a ball and of the assumption that one would foul themselves. Simpson, though, writes that the opposite was true due to the shock, "As all your parts are contracting, you are more likely to be constipated" (Simpson in Fussell 1975, p.49). Soldiers would write poems of the importance of the ration of rum to their daily diet in the trench to calm their nerves, as David Jones recalled:

> O have a care—don't spill the precious
> O don't jog his hand—ministering;
> do take care
> O please—give the poor bugger elbow room.
>
> *(Jones, 1937, p.95)*

Another element that the 'from below' writing allowed was the expansion of perspectives of the war. It was not simply reports to official sources or redacted letters and postcards home. The men would store these memories and use them creatively after they had departed. There was a mysticism and symbolism ascribed to the experience of war from the First World War writers inside the trench. The perspective of both sunrise and sunset seen from below while in the trench would influence the way the sky was interpreted within literature as "emotional climaxes" (Fussell, 1975, p.61) from the ordeals of the day. While these daily markers were significant Romantic rituals, they also heralded the impact of war, when men would come to attention and when Germans could discover the silhouettes of enemies above the trench more easily. It became a period "freighted with implicit aesthetic and moral meaning" (ibid., p.59) and a central theme within British poetry, including Isaac Rosenberg's 'Break of Day in the Trenches':

> The darkness crumbles away.
> It is the same old druid Time as ever,
> Only a live thing leaps my hand,
> A queer sardonic rat,
> As I pull the parapet's poppy
> To stick behind my ear.
> Droll rat, they would shoot you if they knew
> Your cosmopolitan sympathies.
> Now you have touched this English hand
> You will do the same to a German
> Soon, no doubt, if it be your pleasure
> To cross the sleeping green between.
> It seems you inwardly grin as you pass
> Strong eyes, fine limbs, haughty athletes,
> Less chanced than you for life,
> Bonds to the whims of murder,
> Sprawled in the bowels of the earth,
> The torn fields of France.
> What do you see in our eyes
> At the shrieking iron and flame
> Hurled through still heavens?
> What quaver—what heart aghast?
> Poppies whose roots are in man's veins
> Drop, and are ever dropping;
> But mine in my ear is safe—
> Just a little white with the dust.
>
> *(Walter, 2006, p.61)*

These "trench poets" captured popular imagination because suddenly this was not written by poets who also happened to be at war, or by those outside the battle in rushed and titillating novels of "sheer balderdash", as Virginia Woolf called them (ibid., p.8), but from ordinary soldiers. They were isolated in the trenches, yet still writing in a manner that allowed for a closeness that had not been seen before. The trench poetry of the war also allowed the adoption of a much wider variety of poets, where previously publishing opportunities had been reserved for those who approached literacy and literature with a capital 'L', as writes George Walter in *The Penguin Book of First World War Poetry* (ibid., p.10), rather than the common soldier. The styles of Imagism—being precise and radical, and Georgian—less formal, more colloquial and realist, were seen as highly influential in the production of war poetry. Ultimately it was deemed "poetry as reportage" (ibid., p.15) which was as concerned with authenticity as it was with the aesthetics of language of these soldier poets that had a lasting impact:

> We ate our breakfast lying on our backs,
> Because the shells were screeching overhead.
> I bet a rasher to a loaf of bread
> That Hull United would beat Halifax
> When Jimmy Stainthorpe played full-back instead
> of Billy Bradford. Ginger raised his head
> And cursed, and took the bet; and dropt back dead.
> We ate our breakfast lying on our backs,
> Because the shells were screeching overhead.
> *(Wilfred Gibson, 'Breakfast', in Walter, 2006, p.63)*

Tens of thousands of poems were written and set back to magazines, journals, and newspapers during the First World War, though not many have lasted and are still reprinted (Walter, 2006), with this largely being due to subject matter, where the legacy is now around perpetuating the horrors of war and sympathising with those who endured it (ibid., p.25).

White (1987) has previously written about soldiers' notion of themselves in the First World War as tourists in foreign lands and how this provided them with "a protected barrier … precious detachment … to distance themselves from the horrors around them" (ibid., p.71). This idea of detachment and imagined distance is something that conceivably was also encouraged by them reading popular travel literature in the trenches (Fussell, 1975, p.162) to permit imaginative travel beyond the conflict.

In the *Anzac Book*, a collection of Australian and New Zealand writing from the soldiers there are glimpses of the importance of observing place as the soldiers tried to encapsulate their experience, isolated as 'travellers' within foreign countries and within the battle:

> **From My Trench**
>
> A clear, cold night, and in the southern air
> Those far-off thunderings so often there;

A Turkish moon is shining fitfully—
My thoughts are 'neath another moon where we
Paced slowly through the tree stems—you and I.
And, looking back at yon farewell, I sigh
And wonder whether then I cared as much
As now I do when far beyond your touch.
(Cpl. Comus, 2nd Bat., AIF, in Bean, 1916, p.57)

There is also an interesting intersection with travel writing and the writing of war in *Anzac Book*. While there was both physical and cultural isolation, much of the writing 'back home' was a form of travel writing. While these soldiers were cut off from their loved ones and the rest of the world, they were experiencing place in a unique and influential manner.

Fussell notes that it was not just the writing within the trenches that was influential, but also the reading (Fussell, 1980, p.4), where soldiers would fill the time with reading books, especially on travel, for what they hoped to do once the war was over. Sitwell wrote *Discursions on Travel, Art and Life* (1925) as a way to ponder his affection for the orange, the sunny, hot climates where it grows and the difference it provided him from the depravity and cold of his war years. This was also seen with the writing of DH Lawrence, Gerald Brenan, and Alec Waugh, who was so impacted by his time in the freezing trenches in the winter of 1917 that he wrote *Hot Countries* in 1930 about Tahiti, Siam, Ceylon, "and other venues of the palm tree" (Fussell, 1980, p.5) as a response. Waugh's book *The Loom of Youth* about English public-school life in the build-up to the First World War was read in the trenches by Captain HW Yoxall (Fussell, 1980) along with Barbusse's realist *Le Feu* exploring the French soldiers' loathing of the war and *South Wind* by Norman Douglas set on the imaginary island of Nepenthe in the golden Italian sunshine.

Trench journalism and newspapers

While in the First World War there was a "ridiculous proximity" (Fussell, 1975, p.69) not only of the trenches to each other, but also of the distance home for many soldiers across Europe—where it would be only 100 kilometres from a soldier's trench position to the London theatre district in some cases. During the worst of the shelling, French newspaper sellers would still have copies of the *Daily Mail* for troops to read at the end of the trenches only a day after publication. Indeed, there was even publication from within the trenches, with hundreds of papers and newsletters being produced along the line, with British, Australian, Belgian and Canadian periodicals for and by the soldiers being produced. The Germans, Italians, Austrians, and Russians had their own trench papers, along with a prolific contribution from the French (Audoin-Rouzeau, 1992). They ranged in scope from handwritten and crudely sketched (Seal, 2013) through to those with photo reproduction, engravings and copied on printing presses. There was considerable range with the trench presses created; there were newspapers produced by prisoners, the wounded, sailors, airmen, engineers, and troops operating on the Italian and eastern fronts (Audoin-Rouzeau, 1992). The most famous among these was the British paper the *Wipers Times* which was produced by the 'Sherwood foresters' Captain Fred Roberts and Lieutenant Jack Pearson of 12th Battalion who found a damaged printing press in the ruins of the French city Ypres (which they pronounced 'wipers'). The satirical paper often sold in the tens of thousands back in England (Seal, 2013). There were many other trench papers as well, including the *Fifth Gloucester Gazette, The Gasper, The Dead Horse Corner Gazette, The Whizz-Bang*, and *Le Troglodyte*. They would capitalise on this proximity, often having mock advertisements for Christmas hampers and present ideas for the soldier in the trench, such as the advert for "Our Latest Improved Pattern Combination Umbrella and Wire Cutter" in the *Wipers Times* (Fussell, 1975, p.72).

Mainly, the province of the trench press was the "public rather than the private sphere" (Seal, 2013, p.179) where they sought to convey the collective experience of the soldiers in the trenches through sketches, cartoons, verses, songs, and jokes. These presses offered the only writing from the front to back home, while also offering one of the only avenues for "public dialogue" (ibid., p.180) as information from 'home' was transmitted back to the troops as well.

THE
WIPERS TIMES.
OR
SALIENT NEWS.

No 1 Vol I Monday 6th March, 1916. Price 200 Francs.

Are you tired of that hum-drum Existence
—The Existence that Kills—
IF SO
JOIN THE NEW AND GORGEOUSLY APPOINTED
NIGHT CLUB
(NEXT DOOR TO HOTEL DES RAMPARTS.)
And Lead a Gay and Fast Life.

—o—o—o—o—

MANY DARING INNOVATIONS.

—o—o—o—o—

All The Best People Go There.

FIGURE 6.1 Cover of *The Wipers Times*, 6 March 1916
Source: retrieved from Wikimedia Commons, reproduced according to Creative Commons Attribution only licence CC BY 4.0; original image provided by Wellcome Images (library reference RAMC 479, photo number L0031562)

All these literary offerings of war provided something new for readers and writers, a "social observation from a 'bottom-up' perspective", write Chapman and Ellin (2014, p.175) in their article about Dominion satire and trench writing. This also presented the chance to re-consider and expand the historiography of the war to include a 'from below' point of view which could be creative and different from the official accounts.

> Jack and Bill
> Went up a hill
> To see a Frenchman's daughter;
> The Censor's here,
> And so I fear
> I can't say what they taught her.
>
> (The Minden Magazine, *August 1916, cited in Nelson, 2010)*

There were also similar trench presses occurring with the French soldiers further down the line and on the German side, where the soldiers would be dealing with many of the same day-to-day issues as their foes.

Nelson writes that essentially the British contributions would deal with difficult subjects using humour, and the overarching tone would be one of conservatism to justify their position. The French saw no need to justify or defend the conflict and displayed "unflinching honesty" (Nelson, 2010, p.169) with sketches such as that in the January 1916 edition of *Bellica* prominently displaying a nurse on her knees washing the feet of a soldier amputee. The German contribution to trench presses was "by far the largest" (ibid., p.170) in both distribution and the number of papers. The chief concern of these contributions was to justify the war and to defend the 'Fatherland' during the sacrifice the soldiers were making while away from home and invading other countries. This provided the ordinary soldiers with "a language of manly justification for the aggressive and occupational practices of the German Army" (Nelson, 2011, p.1). The German trench papers largely avoided the Nationalist discourse and focused their narratives on the comradeship of those they shared the trenches with and the notion of being a 'good' man and an honest soldier who was warranted in the occupation of Europe. It is important to understand the German perspective to appreciate the voices within the trenches from all sides, "to have a fuller picture of the life-world of German soldiers in the First World War" (ibid., p.3) in order for us to better understand why they fought and what role the trench newspaper played beyond it being simply categorised as the "clumsiest form of propaganda" (ibid.) where it demonstrated the voice beyond the civilian written perspective to reflect on the soldier experience. These German trench papers ranged in readership from 100 up to 130, 000 of a very limited, all male readership living in isolation away from their homes and loved ones (ibid.). These men were trained killers and most coveted the end of the war; their newspapers provided this necessary escapism, often with imagery and sketches of the places they invaded, even appearing as a type of travel writing of the foreign cities and landscapes encountered, while confirming their reasoning for fighting as a defensive and Nationalistic justification for their individual role in the war to make them feel proud "in the midst of horror" (ibid., p.12). One key difference in all these trench newspapers was that while they did operate as propaganda in some sense, they were largely looking for 'good' news and an escape from the realities and politics in the trenches (which could be found in the civilian presses outside the battle). The drawn-out battles, "the combatants' isolation and the need to sustain their morale" (Audoin-Rouzeau, 1992, p.3) brought these newspapers and pamphlets to the surface. The German trench papers were certainly censored (as with the English and French), though the sheer number of them also meant that they offered a more honest depiction of the German soldier psyche and "social reality" (Nelson, 2011, p.5) than any other source.

While there is evidence of all ranks contributing to the trench newspapers of the First World War (Nelson, 2010), the production and writing largely fell to middle-class and lower ranking officers who held jobs in teaching and the humanities outside of the war. Audoin-Rouzeau compiled a comprehensive analysis in *Men at War, 1914–1918: National Sentiment and Trench Journalism in France during the First World War* of the 500 trench press editors he could trace, with two thirds being junior officers, and of the 60 editors with further details, 16 were writers or artists, 13 journalists, 5 lawyers and 4 teachers (Audoin-Rouzeau, 1992). Those who would write and edit the papers were predominantly older soldiers, as the younger men "were more likely to be at the front, running, fighting and dying" (Nelson, 2010, p.171). Across the diversity of trench publishing, beyond the ability to make the soldiers smile or find momentary escapism to travel away for their reality, whether it was British, French, or German, they aimed "to bring all the men together, in solidarity and comradeship" (ibid., p.172) as a reaction to the publishing from their superiors to show pride and loyalty for their cause. The British even named a newspaper the *RMR Growler* to allow soldiers of all ranks to vent their frustrations, whereas the French aim was "to draw tighter still if possible, the ties of friendship which unite them" (Audoin-Rouzeau, 1992, p.14). The German intention was to reinforce the comradeship of their battles in the trenches, especially if they were on the Eastern Front and far from home as a means of self-identification (Nelson, 2010), much the same as the Australians, New Zealanders, and Canadians who also did so in their own trench newspapers being so far from home. The soldiers saw their contribution being to history, and that their 'from below' perspective was providing an alternative narrative of a monumental historical event, where there was not only information, but that a sense of the 'spirit' of the war was recorded, as the Australians wrote in the *Aussie* paper (ibid.).

Comics

A less common, yet equally important demonstration of writing from the trenches came in the form of comic strips and narrative cartoons that would appear in the trench presses as further examples of the participant voices writing from within the Great War

FIGURE 6.2 *Aussie* no. 16, 15 June 1920
Source: reproduced with permission from Museums Victoria

and an early instance of citizen journalism. As Chapman and Ellin (2014) note, it further contributed to this 'bottom up' perspective that the trench newspapers established and allowed for further insight into the daily life, concerns, complaints, and routines while in the trenches as a manner of showing "quick, simple contrasting narratives of shared experiences" (ibid., p.176).

As with many of the British trench papers, the cartoons and comics often relied on humour to explore their specific morality and outlook within the conflict. While cartoons at home often focused on the heroism of the soldiers, the glory of battle and the rhetoric of war (Hiley, 2007), the comics produced in the trenches contained an anti-heroism and irony that fixated on their everyday survival. The comic strips also demonstrated a shared understanding with the Germans across the trenches of what they were all enduring (Ashworth, 1980) and of the absurdity of the situation, such as the Canadian comic on other uses for a bayonet in the trenches, "as a toasting fork, a hook or a corkscrew" (Chapman & Ellin, 2014, p.180). These comic panels published in the trench presses permitted soldiers to vent their frustrations and grievances without it being necessarily official (Cook, 2008) and in a much more immediate sense, when the men in the trenches were often isolated both from home and the larger decisions of their fate.

One of the more important legacies of both the trench newspaper and the comic was the demonstration of autonomy. When so much of the war, and their own lives was out of their control, these writers could push against the propaganda being peddled at home. The writers and cartoonists could regulate the tone of their response and they could choose to boost the morale of those soldiers in the trenches with them as "a symbolic rebellion in cultural expression" (Chapman & Ellin, 2014, p.184).

Nurse writers within the First World War

While traditionally the written account of war, especially from within, has been exclusively male, and privileged to those with combat experience as the "authentic war text" (Nolan, 2007, p.525), the increase in literacy and the appreciation of literature in the First World War was not just a male phenomenon as Fussell (1975) first explored. There was an enormous amount of war writing from the female perspective which was also a "catalyst for creating a unique perspective and for developing a public voice" (Cardinal, 1999, p.1). Most women writers during the First and Second World Wars were nurses, and many, though not all, had come from either writing and publishing or backgrounds in teaching and education. Even when it contravened military orders, many of the nurse writers would write letters and keep diaries for their communities back home and they held the hope of later publication (Hallett, 2016). Sharon Ouditt writes in *Women Writers of the First World War*:

> The very idea that women produced writing about the First World War has often been received with some scepticism. Women, after all, didn't write about the war. They weren't in it. They didn't bear arms, only glimpsed the blood and muck of the battlefields from the shelter of the hospital, and thought plum puddings a Christmas treat rather than a military necessity.
>
> *(Ouditt, 1999, p.1)*

Ouditt charts the important revisioning of this assumption with her annotated bibliography of all the written contributions to the First World War from women. She uncovers and explores the hundreds of novels, magazines, autobiographies, poems, journals and archives written by women in the war who, "literally came under fire from the enemy, and metaphorically from the British military authorities" (ibid., p.1) because of their desire to both make a record of their experiences and to provide an alternative to the male point of view. It is particularly interesting to look at the women of the First World War who wrote 'from below' with as much veracity and immersion as their male counterparts and as a response to the isolation of war to transport their readers into the unique female perspective of the conflict. These accounts would leave an important legacy of their marginalised experiences, while also contributing to the expansion of war writing from those inside it beyond simply trench engagements.

The most prominent example of writing from 'within' in this context and during the war years comes from the nurse writers of the Allies. Unlike their male counterparts who led an outpouring of literary content in the late 1920s and early 1930s, many nurses published memoirs during the war, yet by the 1920s very few of these were available for general readers. Hallett (2016) writes that there has been a re-emergence of the appreciation of the importance of these narratives in recent years. The women's narratives of the First World War helped to demonstrate the diversity of their perspectives from within, with some accepting the heroic notions of war as it was perpetuated back home, while others intentionally challenged the propaganda of these ideas and contributed to new understandings of writing from the First World War due to their unique position of seeing both the anticipation and immediate aftermath of the conflict:

> In caring for those damaged by the First World War, nurses were the most immediate witnesses to the consequences of industrial warfare. Standing between the front lines and the 'home front', and dealing with the worst injuries produced by war, they were ideally placed to witness the results of early-twentieth-century modes of combat.
>
> *(Hallett, 2016, p.5)*

The nurse writers also offered a perspective of the war that had not been seriously considered by the official historians at the time. Only in more recent years with the re-thinking of history (Ankersmit 2001; Jenkins 2003) does the importance of the lived experienced of these women become much more prominent in the understanding of the war experience from inside. In the face of the wave of male writing on the war from 1928 onwards, female nurses such as Vera Brittain published *Testament of Youth* (1933), which gave women a voice in the remembrance of the conflict and the first-hand perspective of the sacrifices made within the war but beyond the trenches. While there was obvious diversity in the many accounts of nurse writers, all were instrumental in "recapturing and recreating experience" (Hallett, 2016, p.10).

One of the more influential and 'unofficial' correspondents from the First World War was nurse and veteran of the South African war Evelyn Kate Luard, who wrote as a response to the gap in stories she saw getting out to the public, initially for her circle of family and friends back home to record her experiences, "with no idea of publication" (Luard, 1915, p.i) but also as a response to the media blackout and the different reality she witnessed caring for thousands of injured soldiers arriving by train at Le Mans and Ypres compared to the 'success' she would read about in *The Times* and the *Daily Mail.* "Frustrated and angered about what she was witnessing in the hospital trains, casualty clearing stations and field hospitals" (McEwen, 2012a, p.8) Luard published *Diary of a Nursing Sister on the Western Front* anonymously in 1915 as a challenge to the heroism of war published by her male counterparts and a reflection on the human cost of the war not seen in the media. Initially she wrote of their journey to Le Havre and of their 'travel experience' of lighthouses, crowded quays in Ireland and a "lovely calm and sunny voyage" (Luard, 1915, p.4), though once she is on duty in Le Mans at the stationary hospital

FIGURE 6.3 An Australian Army nursing sister reading a newspaper to a wounded AIF soldier in a wheelchair at No. 4 AGH (Randwick Military Hospital, later known as the Prince of Wales Hospital)
Source: courtesy of the Australian War Memorial

she writes of the "nasty bread and unripe pears" (ibid., p.37) they have to eat, and then unflinchingly of the cases that are dropped off to them on the trains, "there are some awful mouth, jaw, head, leg, and spine cases, who can't recover, or will only be crippled wrecks. You can't realise that this has all been done on purpose" (ibid., p.39).

As McEwen writes of Luard, "While obviously committed to the men she nursed, she was equally committed to recording their suffering. Furthermore, believing the public had a right to know the human cost of the conflict" (McEwen, 2012b, p.80). She wrote about the horrific casualties they would deal with constantly, at one point there were 12,419 British Expeditionary Force casualties in a ten day stretch in May 1915 yet most of the male superiors would still ignore their contribution to the war effort. Luard's diary was a commercial success, and it received high praise from British papers, *The Daily News* writing "'This diary will tell you more about war than leader writers on impartial prints ever get the chance, worse luck, to learn. From her side of it the nursing sister is a realist'" (cited in McEwen, 2012b, p.82). This was a significant publication from within the isolation of the conflict. It was the first personal account of the initial months of the war published as a book written from the BEF and without approval from the War Office. Despite publishing anonymously, Luard also did this knowing that there could be consequences for her bold move. Ultimately though there were no adverse consequences, as the reality of the war, and the lack of glamour and reward meant that the dwindling numbers of volunteer nurses was a concern, and if the War Office attacked Luard it could have larger implications to challenge the contribution of women, both at the Front and at home. Luard continued to keep a diary of the everyday experiences of being a nurse at war until 1918, and she published the subsequent writing as *Unknown Warriors* (1930) in her own name.

Across north Africa and Europe, Tasmanian nurse May Tilton wrote of her experiences from 1915 to 1919, which were later published as *The Grey Battalion* (1933). Her narrative reads as a style of reportage and even travel as she gives details of her adventure travelling from Launceston in Tasmania to Melbourne, Adelaide then to the unfamiliarity of the rickshaws, cinnamon gardens and beggars with leprosy and elephantiasis in Ceylon. The nurses then arrived in Egypt, which first seemed magical with "brilliant colouring from the heavens above" (Tilton, 1933, p.8) as they travelled across the desert before they encountered death for the first time as injured soldiers were transported in from Gallipoli to be cared for. They began work at the Australian General Hospital in Heliopolis dealing with malaria, shock, and dysentery along with more peculiar problems of their role, such as finding pyjamas for the unusually tall "Queensland patients—men over six feet—wiry, bronzed and healthy when they left home; now sick and weary from months of trench fighting" (ibid., p.17). In between the rush of arriving casualties, the nurses experienced the sights of Egypt, from the incense burners in the narrow streets of Suez, to climbing the pyramids at dusk, the sight of a jackal in between tents, "crouched as though to spring" (ibid., p.37) and witnessing the blessing of the Holy Carpet on its journey to Mecca in a Cairo street in the midst of thousands of locals.

Much of Tilton's writing is concerned with isolation, as they are not only dealing with soldiers coming from the trenches, but they are also largely confined to the casualty clearing stations and makeshift wards when they are not acting as solitary tourists in the streets of Cairo. Once they arrive in Belgium at the British casualty clearing station, Tilton focuses her writing to allow the reader to experience life while under bombardment and battle. The stress of the constant barrages clearly weighs on Tilton as she attempts to get on with her job in the hospital at the front. Each nurse would take turns admitting 200 soldiers at a time. They have morphine at their disposal for the injured, doctors ordered for bromide to be generously administered to patients (Harris, 2008, p.32) along with a steady supply of champagne, stout, brandy and eggs, milk and chicken, "The nearer we were to the guns, the more plentiful were luxuries and noise" (Tilton, 1933, p.250) she remarked of their predicament as fellow nurses would sleep under their beds curled around sandbags to use as comforters. Tilton writes that they would wake to generous cups of black coffee and brandy or cognac to settle their nerves before starting another shift dealing with the consequences of the bombings. Tilton's writing is raw and dramatic, as the medical staff flick the lights out to avoid detection and simultaneously care for injured 'Tommies' while straining to listen to the trajectory of the German bombing planes overhead, without relying on the traditional tropes of heroism for her own part in it. Her writing reflects the no-nonsense nature of her profession, it is clear and impactful for the detail given on life in a frontline hospital.

> A second ear-splitting explosion, nearer; more machine-gun fire from the raider; the barking of our archies; and the Lewis-guns spitting strings of tracer bullets into the air, added to the pandemonium. A nerve-racked lad clung to me in terror. I endeavoured to calm his fears and begged him to wait a moment while I ran round the beds in the dark so the patients would know I was there with them.
>
> *(Tilton, 1933, p.252)*

Tilton calms the soldier, whose leg has also just been amputated, though there is barely space to breath before a new load of soldiers suffering from mustard gas exposure arrive.

Women's writing from this period also saw important developments in tone and style, as the written experience of women in war previously had "few literary models which were specific to their experience" (Cardinal 1999, p.7). By not being chiefly concerned with recounting the battles, it also allowed space to reconsider what war writing could be, presenting a stylistic break from what had come before. Nurse writers were influential in the change of how women writers were appreciated more broadly, with some seen as accidental modernists and avant-garde for how they attempted to make sense of the conflict. Many accounts would promote pacificism or question the rhetoric of war because of the sympathy attached to their accounts as writers who would "bear witness to the suffering and courage" (Hallett, 2016, p.10) they saw all around them. Many of the accounts from nurse writers helped make sense of what was occurring and acted as a survival mechanism for the writers to reassemble what had happened. These new experiences narrated the experience of women in conflict as had not been witnessed previously with "self-awareness and confidence in being alert chroniclers of their part in the conflict. Therefore narratives relating to the excitement and exhilaration of war are as indicative as those which speak of loneliness, anguish, and bereavement" (Ouditt, 1999, p.2). Tilton's writing gives further evidence of this point when we learn of her time in Poperinghe at the casualty clearing station on 4 October 1917. She moved from fractured arm, to haemorrhaging soldier, to shattered jaw, still with the foresight to reflect on the imperative that while the understood agreement was for all British soldiers to be seen before Germans, in practice she was happy to treat German prisoners of war (Harris, 2008, p.32), especially when they were in the midst of the pain, and the screams and the blood of the soldiers, "less serious cases of British soldiers were often kept waiting while the more seriously wounded Germans were treated and cared for" she wrote (Tilton, 1933, p. 260).

In Peter Rees's *Anzac Girls: The Extraordinary Story of our World War 1 Nurses* (2008) he writes from diaries and journals of five nurses from Australia and New Zealand as they were stationed in Gallipoli, on the Western Front and on the Aegean Islands.

In one anecdote, a group of mainly New Zealand nurses were aboard the *Marquette* ship on its way to Thessaloniki when it was sunk on 23 October 1915 by a German submarine. The large troopship was transporting nurses among the soldiers, though it did not carry a Red Cross flag, which rendered it vulnerable to attack. Torpedos hit the ship in the early morning and among the 167 dead were 10 New Zealand nurses.

Surviving New Zealand nurse Jeannie Sinclair wrote of the experience of floating on debris after the attack:

> It was dreadful to see some of the other men going whitey-yellow and then blue around the nose, mouth and eyes and, a little later, passing out. One man, who died early in the morning, floated with us all day.
>
> *(Cited in Rees 2008, p.129)*

These accounts demonstrated that the women nurse writers were undoubtedly as close to harm as any male soldier's experience of the war, yet the nurses also wrote of the medical impact with understanding and sincerity not often seen in male accounts of the conflict.

While venereal disease became increasingly prevalent for soldiers on their days off, with 2000 Australian soldiers alone infected in early 1915 (Rees, 2008), the male and official perspective either wrote about it as a laugh, or as grounds for moral panic, whereas the nurses showed compassion and understanding. Sister Alice Ross King in Cairo railed against the hysteria, an opinion even seen in some of her sister superiors who refused to treat infected men, "I'm really longing to nurse that man and perhaps save his eyesight. This wretched woman made a fuss and would not go in the boys' tent—I could slay her" wrote King in her diary at the time (cited in Rees 2008, p.29).

The resonance of the nurse's stories in popular culture and writing has also continued into the 21st century, with the adaptation of Rees's book for the 2013 series *Anzac Girls* on ABC television. In an era where the female perspective was once again being superseded by the male and heroic point of view with series such as *Band of Brothers* (2001) and *The Pacific* (2010) this offered "an alternative history about the war that privileges women's experiences" (Packard & Stubbs, 2016, p.109).

As an example of how war was written about from within with intimacy and authority, without it necessarily detailing the blow-by-blow details of battle, the women would devote much of their writing to issues which were rarely spoken about. As Packard and Stubbs write:

> The Australian Army saw venereal disease as a moral issue rather than a medical one, and the tens of thousands of men who became infected were regarded by High Command as 'rotten' and 'swindlers' with their pay stopped for the duration of their absence from duty.
>
> *(Packard & Stubbs, 2016, p.113)*

The expansion of perspective from the nurses allowed these themes to be addressed with seriousness and sensitivity.

Women journalists and war correspondents

One of the more obvious outlets for writing from within a war comes from the journalists who are sent to cover the conflicts. The objectivity, importance, and ethics of these reporters as they tell the stories of war has been written about from many angles. There has been a long-held fascination with war correspondents and their writing transporting the reader into battle while also examining its impact, yet this has largely centred on men and what they have written. Women war correspondents remain largely forgotten when compared to their more remembered and celebrated male colleagues.

From an international perspective, female war correspondents go back to the US–Mexico war in 1846 when "Jane McManus Storms, writing under the pseudonym of Cora Montgomery for the *New York Sun*, went behind enemy lines in order to file her first-hand dispatches" (McEwen, 2012a, p.2). At the time she was the only female journalist covering the conflict, and likely she was the very first female war correspondent. In Australia, the first female war correspondent was Agnes Macready who reported on the South African War in 1900 for the *Catholic Press*.

During the First World War, women journalists were often only permitted to cover items of 'women's interest', largely the social and economic aspects of the conflict, with only a select few "reporting from the front" (McEwen, 2012a, p.3).

By the Second World War women were accredited, alongside men, to cover the conflict. In Australia, however, despite their being twenty-one women war correspondents in the conflict, the Australian Army accredited them for "the express purpose of publicising women's work on the home front" (Baker, 2015a, p.166) while both Australian and European authorities sought to control the writing of women correspondents by restricting their access to the military zone.

Vera Brittain, who published the influential *Testament of Youth* (1933), was a nurse and a writer in the First World War, and embarked on a second career as a journalist and correspondent for the subsequent world conflict, with Badsey noting that "her writing in the Second World War was both insightful and valuable, recording especially the experience of ordinary people on the home front in detail and from a unique perspective" (Badsey, 2012, p.140). Brittain travelled to Germany in 1936 as a journalist to cover the rise of Nazism first-hand and saw the cycle of wars she had lived through would only be broken through pacifist ideals and practical action of which her writing embodied. Partly because of her influence from the First World War and her undoubted patriotism she was allowed to publish *England's Hour* (1941) about the Battle of Britain and the Blitz with a tone that called for understanding, balance and wider-ranging sympathy, Germans included, hallmarks of what many of the women nurses writing in the First World War had reflected upon. She would later publish books and pamphlets furthering her pacifist beliefs including *Humiliation with Honour* (1942), *One of These Little Ones … A Plea to Parents and Others for Europe's Children* (1943) and *Seed of Chaos: What Mass*

Bombing Really Means (1944) in the hope of prompting readers, who ranged from ordinary people to US President Roosevelt, to question the consequences and lasting impact of war. Brittain's writing was received with hostility in England for its criticism of British military strategy, even from George Orwell in the *Tribune* (Badsey, 2012, p.144), yet it was a success in the United States for its honest perspective and care for what would happen post-war:

> These orators and broadcasters who treat war as though it were a blood sport and describe it in terms of a cup-tie final, do not represent the spirit of ordinary British men and women who offer cups of tea to crashed German pilots or go out to rescue them in small boats when they fall into the Channel.
> *(Brittain, 1981 [1941], p.38)*

For Australian journalist Lorraine Stumm to gain access to the Second World War she continually pestered military authorities while she wrote for London's *Daily Mirror*, though she was often met with all manner of excuses, including the lack of female toilets in operational areas (Baker, 2015a). When Stumm was working as a general reporter after the war, she travelled to Japan (at her own expense) and she got an important scoop, an interview with Father Wilhelm Kleinsorge in a Tokyo hospital, the first known European survivor of the Hiroshima bombing. Kleinsorge would end up being one of the most important interviewees in John Hersey's *New Yorker* article and later book titled *Hiroshima* (1946) which was seen as the birth of New Journalism. In Stumm's interview with Kleinsorge, conducted before Hersey's, it was noteworthy as it gave a voice to survivors on the ground when nearly all other discussion of the atomic bombings was censored.

The acknowledgement of the importance of women's war journalism is gradually changing, with works such as those by Ouditt, Badsey, Baker, and McKewen, though for a long time the importance of this alternative view of what it is like to be confined within a war from a female perspective has been ignored and submerged in the more prevalent narrative, that men told the stories of war, and were even invited to march in commemorations (Baker, 2015a), while women "who covered World War II were not 'proper' war correspondents" (Baker, 2015b, p.40).

Writing and isolation beyond the battlefield

One of the most well-known and tragic examples of writing and confinement related to any theme within this book is surely *Anne Frank: The Diary of a Young Girl* (Frank, 2002 [1947]). While the Frank family story from their Second World War confinement is well known, in the context of this book it is also worth revisiting the details and the significance of both her diary and Kitty, her imaginary friend the journal was written for.

As Barnouw writes in *The Phenomenon of Anne Frank*, "Anne Frank as a writer easily reached the twenty-first century. Her diary continues to be translated, and its sales continue undiminished; her place of hiding now draws more than one million visitors per year" (Barnouw, 2018, p.112).

Anne Frank was the youngest daughter of Otto and Edith Frank, from a middle-class German Jewish family who were forced to relocated from Frankfurt to Amsterdam in 1933–1934 with the rise of the Nazi party. As the restrictions increased on the Jews, the family was left little choice but to make decisions to prolong their survival. Initially Otto tried to emigrate from the Netherlands, though eventually their only option was to move into a hidden annexe at the back of the factory he was the former owner of, before Jews were prevented from owning businesses altogether in 1940 (Frank, 2002 [1947]). The diary begins on 12 June 1942, her birthday, when Frank is given it as a gift by her parents and they move into their new hiding place only a few weeks later.

Frank is sure initially that no one would be interested in the musings of a 13-year-old stuck in a warehouse annexe. "I want the diary to be my friend, and I'm going to call this friend *Kitty*" (Frank, 2002 [1947], p.13) she writes. The families share the space, spread over five narrow floors and with an entrance concealed by a purpose-built bookshelf with the van Pels family and later with the dentist Fritz Pfeffer. For the first year or so, 'Kitty' provides an outlet for Frank as she adjusts to their routines and the uncertainty of the future. With so little variation in their lives, 'Kitty' allows Frank to vent in private and to make sense of her place in the annexe.

Much of the diary is concerned with the interactions and observations of the others in the annexe with Frank. There is constant bickering, passive aggressive encounters, frustrations, and despair at their situation as they are all trapped inside day after day, season after season. As many of us have come to appreciate in the current pandemic, there are also instant mood swings and changes of opinion as they're confined to the annexe. As an interesting aside on the 'writing' of the experience, Frank amends diaries later with comments in italics to further contextualise her thoughts and the spur of the moment feelings she has, in particular with those entries related to her mother and her realisation of the fracture in their relationship and the difference in their personalities. On one day, Frank writes about Pfeffer (named 'Albert Dussel' in the diary), her roommate, and how his selfishness and bad attitude are grating on her: "My plans for revenge, such as unscrewing the light bulb, locking the door and hiding his clothes, have unfortunately had to be abandoned in the interest of peace" (Frank, 2002 [1947], p.104). Then, with the next entry, this bickering is forgotten as they are aware of what is happening in Amsterdam outside their hiding place: "Terrible things are happening outside. At any time of night and day, poor helpless people are being dragged out of their homes" (ibid., p.105). Despite 'Kitty' being Frank's sanctuary, what is clear from her writing is her optimism for herself and their future, even if it is naïve, there is something we can all appreciate about her positivity, "being on holiday in some strange pension" (ibid., p.37) as she quips, rather than spiralling into depression as it seems the adults do intermittently.

As a novel example of close travel, and a further demonstration of Frank's imagination and positive outlook, in late 1942 she decides to 'travel' to Switzerland with her father. They redecorate the apartment they're sharing with Frank's cousins, and she then goes on an imaginary shopping trip buying pyjamas, winter and summer shoes, scarves, belts, handbags, ice skates, and suntan lotion among many other items. This transportation offers a respite, and a window into the importance of creative thought in her circumstances, before she transitions once again to the realities of the Gestapo, ration cards, and cramped living conditions.

In the most impactful event of her time in the annexe, Frank eventually falls in love with Peter, the young son of the van Pels (re-named the van Daans in the book) and what makes this such as intriguing example of isolation writing is the importance of her diary in processing the relationship. Frank struggles with the day-to-day of living with the uncertainty (as they all do), and as she realises that her feelings for Peter are growing, even though he is mere metres away in their hiding space and not in another suburb or from a different school as this might have played out in 'normal' circumstances. Frank invents reasons to bump into him, she hopes that he'll seek her out and she retreats to her diary to untangle her thoughts, "Oh, Peter, if only you could hear me or see me" (Frank, 2002 [1947], p.248), she writes.

Reading this now during COVID-19 it gives readers a new appreciation not only for Frank's discipline in writing the diary, but also a deeper understanding of the irritability, even when it is irrational, of living in close proximity to others for weeks on end.

> It all boils down to this: whenever one of the eight of us opens his mouth, the other seven can finish the story for him. We know the punch line of every joke before it gets told, so that whoever's telling it is left to laugh alone.
>
> *(Frank, 2002 [1947], pp.226–227)*

While part of the reading of the diary can be appreciated for its innocence and naivety, reading her diary and the sense of hope and ambitions she possesses despite their horrible reality is a salve for readers in the 21st century and a chance to appreciate the determination in a manner we may not have been able to prior to our own COVID experiences.

There is a real sense of both power and relatability to Frank's diary and the writing of their experiences of hiding in much the same way we see all the writers in this collection telling their own stories. It is an example of the agency she possessed, ownership of her developing understanding of herself and their predicament. It is also a demonstration of her compassion for the others in the annexe as they grow together in this strange environment and an important legacy for the war as experienced by a 13-year-old Jewish girl in Amsterdam as we readers now filter this through our COVID experiences. Frank's writing is unique in this collection for the manner in which she grew during her time in confinement: she matured as a daughter, sister and friend; she developed her love for writing; she read on everything from biographies of Hungarian composers to botany, history, and *An Ideal Husband*; she fell in love with Peter and developed a strong sense of her own worth; all while being confined the annexe with seven others.

Only days before they are discovered and arrested, Frank writes on 15 July 1944:

> I feel the suffering of millions. And yet, when I look up at the sky, I somehow feel that everything will change for the better, that this cruelty too will end, that peace and tranquillity will return once more. In the mean time, I must hold on to my ideals. Perhaps the day will come when I'll be able to realize them!
>
> *(Frank, 2002 [1947], p.419)*

In one of her final statements, we witness the way she has changed through her period in isolation. Somehow despite the despair, love, helplessness, bickering and being trapped in the small annexe she maintains hope until the end. As Barnouw confirms, "it is Anne's optimistic and lively side that will attract new readers and new visitors. The phenomenon of Anne Frank will continue on" (Barnouw, 2018, p.116).

After nearly two years in the annexe with the seven others and Kitty, they were finally discovered on 4 August 1944 by the SS and Dutch security police. It's still not known if they were ultimately betrayed by workers in the factory, though they were transferred to a detention centre in Weteringschans in Amsterdam and then to Westerbork, the "Jewish transit camp" on the very last transport to the extermination camp (Frank, 2002 [1947], p.427). Of the eight in the annexe, only Otto Frank survived, with Anne Frank and her sister Margot both dying of typhus in the Bergen-Belsen concentration camp between February and March 1945, only weeks before it was liberated by British troops.

'Kitty' survived the initial arrest, with Miep Gies, one of the people who had helped the families in the annexe, collecting Frank's diary on the day they were taken. She eventually returned it to Otto Frank, with the first version of the diary published in 1946.

* * *

Fussell wrote that modes of remembrance that are "illuminated by emotion" (Fussell, 1975, p.338) such as the writing from these confined and isolated soldiers, nurses and citizens has the greatest potential to endure. What we may garner from this theme of war and confinement in the context of COVID-19 is not only how powerful the writing is written from within conflict, to find deeper meaning and to push through fear and uncertainty, but also how important this writing is as a vestige of what these people saw, felt and dreamed of when in these circumstances. What I also think it alerts us to reading it through our own period of isolation is the importance of writing in all forms. Many of the examples in this chapter where never initially intended for publication, so there is a simplicity to the observations which has authenticity—of the importance of rum in the trenches, the small victories of dry boots, or hot coffee, of the many ways to cook potatoes as per Anne Frank, and the slow realisation of falling in love in the most unlikely environment. This is what I hope might be learned from our COVID-19 period behind closed doors and shut borders, that people might write in journals, construct poems, jot down emails and begin novels so as to refine the feelings of enduring this pandemic so that we might look back on it and appreciate what it was to be present in this moment, to critique it and to distil it for the future.

The re-emergence of the various written perspectives from below, of Anne Frank, of soldiers within the trenches and pacifist nurses offer a more complicated perspective of history and its usefulness across a variety of genres and experiences. Indeed only a few years ago it would have seemed absurd to take comfort and instruction on how to deal with a pandemic's lockdown from a soldier in 1914 in the Somme or a 13-year-old Jewish girl from 1940s Amsterdam.

While the world wars were almost universal in their impact, the writing from 'within' the isolation and confinement also demonstrates their great range. From the multi-million dollar industry that has come about from Anne Frank's diary to the broad impact of war poetry and the recognition of the 'from below' perspective in allowing readers to travel inside the experience with intimacy and authenticity. The writing of war has also shown the diversity of literary impact and influence, of the importance of journalism, diaries, satire, comics and of the modern renditions inspired by these narratives which encompass everything from computer games and VR experiences to stage plays and Netflix animations to continually reflect on the legacy of writing, isolation, and conflict.

References

Ankersmit, F 2001, *Historical Representation*. Stanford University Press.

Ashworth, T (1980) *Trench Warfare 1914–18: The Live and Let Live System*. The Macmillan Press.

Audoin-Rouzeau, S (1992). *Men at War, 1914–1918: National Sentiment and Trench Journalism in France during the First World War*. Berg.

Badsey, P (2012). *Vera Brittain: War Reporter 1939–1945*. In Y McEwen & FA Fisken (eds), War, Journalism and History. Peter Lang UK.

Baker, J (2015a). War stories: Remembering women conflict reporters. *Griffith Review*, 48, 165–181.

Baker, J (2015b). Marginal Creatures: Australian Women War Reporters During World War II. *History Compass*, 13(2), 40–50.

Barnouw, D (2018). *The Phenomenon of Anne Frank* (trans. JK Ringold). Indiana University Press.

Bean, CEW (ed.) (1916). *The Anzac Book: Written and Collected in Gallipoli by the Men of Anzac*. Cassell.

Brittain, V (1981 [1941]). *England's Hour: An Autobiography 1939–1941*. Futura.

Cardinal, A (1999). Introduction. In A Cardinal, D Goldman, & J Hattaway (eds), *Women's Writing on the First World War*. Oxford University Press.

Chapman, C & Ellin, D (2014). Dominion cartoon satire as trench culture narratives: Complaints, endurance and stoicism. *The Round Table*, 103(2), 175–192.

Cook, T. (2008). Anti-heroes of the Canadian expeditionary force. *Journal of the Canadian Historical Association*, 19(1), 171–193.

Darnton, R (1984). *The Great Cat Massacre and Other Episodes in French Cultural History*, Basic Books.

Frank, A (2002 [1947]). *Diary of a Young Girl. Penguin Classics.*

Fussell, P (1975). *The Great War and Modern Memory. Oxford University Press.*

Fussell, P (1980). *Abroad: British Literary Traveling between the Wars. Oxford University Press.*

Ginzburg, C (1980). *The Cheese and the Worms: The Cosmos of a Sixteenth-Century Miller, Johns Hopkins University Press.*

Hallett, CE (2016). *Nurse Writers of the Great War. Manchester University Press.*

Harris, K. (2008). In the 'grey battalion': Launceston General Hospital nurses on active service in World War I. *Health and History*, 10(1), 21–40.

Hersey, J (2006 [1946]). *Hiroshima. Penguin Books.*

Hiley, N (2007). A new and vital morale factor: Cartoon book publishing during the First World War. In M Hammondand & S Towheed (eds), *Publishing in the First World War.* Basingstoke: Palgrave Macmillan, pp. 148–177.

Jenkins, K (2003). *Rethinking History*. Psychology Press.

Jones, D (1937). *In Parenthesis*. Faber & Faber.

Luard, E (1915). *Diary of a Nursing Sister on the Western Front.* William Blackwood and Sons.

McEwen, Y (2012a). Introduction. In Y McEwen & FA Fisken (eds), *War, Journalism and History*. Peter Lang UK.

McEwen, Y (2012b). Behind and between the lines: The war diary of Evelyn Kate Luard, nursing sister. In Y McEwen & FA Fisken (eds), *War, Journalism and History*. Peter Lang UK.

Nelson, RL (2010). Soldier newspapers: A useful source in the social and cultural history of the First World War and beyond. *War in History*, 17(2), 167–191.

Nelson, RL (2011). *German Soldier Newspapers of the First World War.* Cambridge University Press.

Nolan, E (2007). American women writers and the First World War. *Literature Compass*, 4, 525–538.

Ouditt, S (1999). Women writers of the First World War. In *Women Writers of the First World War: An Annotated Bibliography* (1st ed.). Taylor & Francis Group.

Packard, F, & Stubbs, B (2016). ANZAC girls: An ethical autoanalysis. In S Maras, *Ethics in Screenwriting: New Perspectives*. Palgrave Macmillan, pp. 99–123.

Rees, P (2008). *Anzac Girls: The Extraordinary Story of Our World War 1 Nurses.* Allen & Unwin.

Seal, G (2013). 'We're here because we're here': Trench culture of the Great War. *Folklore (London)*, 124(2), 178–199.

Tilton, M (1933). *The Grey Battalion*. Angus & Robertson.

Walter, G (ed.) (2006). *The Penguin Book of First World War Poetry*. Penguin Books.

White, R (1987). The soldier as tourist: The Australian experience of the Great War. *War & Society*, 5(1): 63–77.

7

WRITING AND COVID-19

"Hell is other people", said Jean-Paul Sartre's character Garcin in the play *No Exit* (Sartre, 1958, p.26), when he realised that despite being in 'purgatory', hell was not some place of furnaces, devils, and whips, but an endless loop of time with three conflicting characters trapped together in a windowless drawing room for eternity. Despite the statement's convenience in the COVID era to remind us of the amount of time we've had to spend in confinement with no company other than our loved (or sometimes not so loved) ones during lockdowns in much the same way that Garcin, Inez, and Estelle do in *No Exit*, Sartre meant something else. He was exploring the notion that we seek validation for our choices, good, bad, or otherwise through other people; we are defined through the gaze of others and their judgement of our lives.

No Exit is interesting to consider and to re-visit during the pandemic as an absurdist take on the search for meaning from within lockdown. Just like the characters in Sartre's play, we've all spent an inordinate amount of time in various forms of isolation without a clear idea of why or how it might conclude. As Garcin says when they are grappling with their situation in isolation, "I'd rather be alone. I want to think things out, you know; to set my life in order, and one does that better by oneself. But I'm sure we'll manage to pull along together somehow" (Sartre, 1958, p.6), however despite the positive intentions, within moments Inez is fixated on Garcin and his irritable tendency to gyrate his mouth when he speaks. The characters eventually realise that in the absence of an 'official' torturer, they're placed in isolation together to act as tormentors for one another, "The same idea as in the cafeteria, where customers serve themselves" (ibid., p.10) quips Inez.

The ability to reconcile the meaning to be taken from COVID's enforced lockdowns has been difficult for many as we negotiate shared space while still being closed in, as with Sartre's protagonists, with no concrete idea of when, or if, the status quo we find ourselves within will end and what we might appear like at the other end of it.

DOI: 10.4324/9781003243267-7

In the months and years to come, as we seek to find greater meaning from our COVID-19 experiences, not only is the parable behind *No Exit* valid, but it also offers an opportunity to see how creativity and meaning might be discovered from this period through writing. Over the last two years many of us no doubt have also felt like Garcin, Inez, and Estelle—left in the confines of a room to work out how we'll endure the endless twists of lockdown. In the contemporary context I believe it is our creative responses to the imposed isolation which can demonstrate meaning for the pandemic's lasting impact. While many have had periods of apathy and inactivity, there have also been great sparks of inspiration generated by the isolation borne from COVID.

During the enforced COVID confinement of 2020–2022, has being isolated and 'trapped' with only a select few people been something that has stifled creativity and writing, or is the urge to create more significant than this impediment? While in some circumstances I think that hell certainly can be other people, the pandemic has also demonstrated our inherent need to share our work, to continue writing, to address the frailties of the world in creative ways and to write through the most significant confinement of our time as a way to make sense of it and to also capture the feelings of being within it.

Time to keep writing

As soon as the seriousness of the pandemic was understood, it forced the closure of writing and literature festivals around the world, bookshops shut their doors, music performances and live entertainment was curtailed and suddenly all we had was our bookshelves, our computer screens, and our imaginations for creative company.

To demonstrate the importance of sharing stories irrespective of the barrier imposed, it didn't take long for those at the helms of the various festivals celebrating writing to pivot to a new way of sharing stories.

The Jaipur Literature Festival, as the largest literature festival in the world, with multiple offerings beyond its flagship India event, moved online quickly for its festivals in Ireland, the US, Australia, and the UK (along with new iterations of the Indian version) where a suite of online events were curated, 'JLF Brave New World' and the 'Words are Bridges' festival brought in 416 speakers and reached 5 million views online through curated streaming events and recorded podcasts.

In New Zealand, a country that has fared better than most in this period of instability, the 'Word Christchurch' event sold out, despite the COVID restrictions constraining numbers and space, as they decided to focus on the near-at-hand by only featuring local authors and local issues in their programme (Gates, 2020).

In Asia there were sweeping impacts on the festival circuit, though there have been more options for online engagement than ever before. As Partogi and Emilia (2020) write in the *Jakarta Post*, "Makassar International Writers Festival (MIWF) in Makassar, South Sulawesi; Jakarta International Literary Festival (JILF) in Jakarta;

and Bali's Ubud Writers and Readers Festival (UWRF)" all ceased in-person offerings but still conducted online festivals, thus connecting many writers and readers from countries around Asia and the region who might not have otherwise ventured to a writing event, even pre COVID. Despite this band-aid, the evidence of inequality, especially when it comes to internet and technological access has become clear, highlighting that while this may be a way to navigate through the uncertainty momentarily, it's certainly not a way to expand the reach of discussions on writing and creativity for good.

The Melbourne Writers Festival in 2021 ran with the theme 'Tell me how it ends' to funnel the lockdown experience through the guests and their responses. The festival utilised many pre-recorded talks with authors to elongate the festival experience, fostering a digital intimacy on the screen between writers and readers that at least allowed for a conversation and a dialogue to continue even if there was a falsity to the perceived closeness.

In the UK, the Ledbury Poetry Festival not only ran online sessions as with the Jaipur Literature Festival, they also curated a specific lockdown poems section for direct response to the pandemic and hosted a community patchwork craft event for those either not keen, or unable to engage online, linking all those in lockdown along a 500 mile trail with the common cause of action against climate change, where artists brought together "stitched griefs, remembrances, prayers and hopes connected to their local landscapes and stories of migration" (Coat of Hopes, 2021).

Writers' centres, such as Writers South Australia that I am involved with, ran online workshops and writing sessions with national and international authors that they never would have been able to book previously. Importantly, it also levelled the playing field so that aspiring writers outside capital cities could access the same content and privileges as their urban counterparts.

These sorts of creative responses have happened before and it suggests that innovation and re-thinking is constantly occurring in these creative spaces, as Michaela McGuire notes of Behrouz Boochani's presentation at the Sydney Writers Festival in 2019 while he was still incarcerated on Manus Island:

> It was also one of the fastest-selling. That was really encouraging, knowing that audiences were willing to do something a little different. And, if the main attraction isn't in the room, there's still something really powerful about having a large group of audience members together, experiencing an event at the same time.
>
> *(McGuire, 2020)*

Despite the hope, ingenuity, and positive responses that have come during the pandemic, it's not all optimistic though, as Rajan (2020) writes. The pandemic led to the inevitable closure of many creative outlets that were propped up by unsustainable business models, including magazines, publishing companies and newspapers, and many others that have slimmed down and moved online permanently. Poliakova (2021) writes that while 58 per cent of Canadians reported reading more during lockdown, Indigo, Canada's largest bookseller was forced to close 20 locations, undoubtedly with readers syphoned to Amazon and similar platforms for their convenience when people were rendered immobile. Similarly, in Australia there was a 13 per cent rise in fiction sales in 2020, with a clear increase of people focusing their literature on their own cities and regions, another example of the usefulness of the 'near-at-hand'. On the downside, new authors who normally rely on the publicity of interviews, signings, festivals and in-person contact to garner initial interest and attention for their new writing have lost out to many of the bigger and more established names in publishing.

While it is undoubted that COVID has provided a circuit breaker for the publishing, book-selling and festival industries, as Smart writes, "It is likely that we will feel the effect of the financial and practical outcomes of this pandemic for several years. However, it has provided the opportunity for increased collaboration, innovation, and the embracing of a 'new normal'" (Smart, 2020).

O'Connor also writes that this reset should give writers, readers and publishers an opportunity to recalibrate some entrenched imbalances in the industry to focus on the importance of local perspectives, on the inequalities of racism and structural bias still present within the writing and publishing industries, and a chance to revaluate the importance of "openness, transparency, and trust" in all forms of nonfiction writing (O'Connor, 2021).

Beyond O'Connor's prompt for where new publishing and writing can explore these important areas in greater depth, what the pandemic does in an optimistic sense is to allow for a pause so writers might consider the long-held question of 'why they write' once again. Sullivan noted the sombre tone at the 2021 Melbourne Writers Festival in this vein, and of author Sigrid Nunez's approach, that living in this state of pandemic grief might prompt us to do nothing, but it can also be enormously conducive and inspirational, living within an event as big and all-encompassing as the pandemic has been:

> One of her characters says that if every poet wrote about the climate crisis, it would not save one tree. "But it's not the poet's job to save trees." And yet she still feels some sense of obligation. "On the one hand it feels like it's too soon to be writing about the pandemic. But on the other hand you feel you shouldn't be writing about anything else."
>
> *(Sullivan, 2021)*

It could be argued that during lockdown, when you're in the sanctuary of a home office, or a kitchen bench with earphones on to block out the home schooling occurring in the other room as you wait out the days, it is a wonderful opportunity to now consider the question 'why we write' that Joan Didion and George Orwell have prompted many readers and aspiring writers to consider in the past.

Orwell wrote in his essay 'Why I write' in 1946 of his early compulsion to be creative and that the war-time era he grew up in was inescapably interlinked with his desire to seek out and to tell stories due to its vivacity:

> I do not think one can assess a writer's motives without knowing something of his early development. His subject-matter will be determined by the age he lives in—at least this is true in tumultuous, revolutionary ages like our own.
>
> *(Orwell, 2021 [1946], p.15)*

Interestingly, the world wars and era of instability Orwell was referring to for his own writing development have some similarities to our pandemic times now. And may well influence new writers in the same way the war experience influenced writers of Orwell's era.

Thirty years after Orwell, Joan Didion borrowed the same title, 'Why I write' for her essay in the *New York Times* to ponder how this question manifested itself in a different country and an altogether different period. Didion's response wasn't focused on the philosophies of her ideas or their abstract manifestations, she was interested in the minutia of her life, to utilise the phrase I have used many times in this book—on the near-at-hand—around her as she was working out what inspired her and captured her attention. Rather than focusing on the academic details during her formative university years she was more interested in the sensory particulars of her everyday life and how she could express these.

> I can still recall the exact rancidity of the butter in the City of San Francisco's dining car, and the way the tinted windows on the Greyhound bus cast the oil refineries around Carquinez Straits into a grayed and obscurely sinister light. In short my attention was always on the periphery, on what I could see and taste and touch, on the butter, and the Greyhound bus.
>
> *(Didion, 1976, p.276)*

Didion realised that her focus on these sensory details gave her the answer to a question she wasn't sure she was even asking yet, that she was a writer, "a person whose most absorbed and passionate hours are spent arranging words on pieces of paper" (ibid., p.276). The awareness of the details of her life and what inspired her was instructive for Didion, she realised that writing helped her "to find out what I'm thinking, what I'm looking at, what I see and what it means. What I want and what I fear" (ibid., p.276). There is also value in Didion's realisation from nearly 50 years ago that I think resonates now during the pandemic, where it can allow new writers and those looking to re-think their craft to appreciate a period of introspection and 're-tooling' of the genres and styles they are normally drawn towards.

Sometimes this discovery of wanting to be a writer or realising that there are different ways of accessing the stories in your head can come from having the sort of elongated puddles of time that the pandemic has allowed.

Time to be idle

Pico Iyer wrote in *The Art of Stillness: Adventures in Going Nowhere*:

> Sitting still as a way of falling in love with the world and everything in it; I'd seldom thought of it like that. Going nowhere as a way of cutting through the noise and finding fresh time and energy to share with others.
>
> *(Iyer, 2014, p.4)*

It is only after enduring lockdowns ourselves that we can appreciate Iyer's words for their usefulness to our current (and future) motivations for writing and how the inactivity of the pandemic can offer a valuable sense of focus and re-thinking for our craft.

Hobart-based author Robert Dessaix extended Iyer's impression of stillness and he further addressed the way we treat 'spare' time in his 2017 book, *The Pleasures of Leisure* and how we might 'use' this time to ponder questions such as that first asked by Orwell. Dessaix's claim was that so few of us possess a "talent" for enjoying time not filled by work and productive commitments, yet it is something we should be able to do, and not just because of a pandemic. Dessaix provides a fascinating treatise on idleness and how we might better approach and embrace it. Dessaix's words are particularly apt now; he wrote in 2017 that "There is a disquiet spreading rapidly across the globe about empty time" (Dessaix, 2017, p.2) It could just as easily have been written in 2021 about the scores of people doing their best during lockdown (or those compelled to break the rules because they don't know how to be idle). There is something to reflect on in Dessaix's words during the current period as one thing many writers, and people in general have more of, is time.

Dessaix prompted the reader to ask what they want from their spare time. He also challenged us to think about what leisure means—is it entertainment, a hobby, a sport or simply being idle? When so much of our time is monetised and categorised, being able to separate these activities out and to not attach a sense of guilt to our free time is increasingly important. Dessaix contends that well spent idleness becomes a form of mindfulness, "a kind of vigorous, centred inactivity" (Dessaix, 2017, p.14) that allows us to learn to be at home with and to figure out important aspects of ourselves.

Dessaix's chapter on 'Nesting' is particularly useful during the pandemic. He takes us to the rubbish tip of all places to explore the importance of enjoying our own space, whether that's throwing out broken garden equipment across a sea of garbage, as Dessaix does to allow him to embrace his *new* garden, or pruning trees, brushing the dog, playing the piano, having sex, or mending socks. If these activities are done for the joy they afford and not the usefulness of the action, it allows us to appreciate the pleasures of leisure as he intends. I would extend Dessaix's ideas of idleness to also allow us to consider creativity more fundamentally, to think about why we write, why we read and other ways we might find the same fulfilment to allow us to tap back into those initial reasons we had for pursuing writing in the first place. Time, concluded Dessaix, was for magnifying your humanity and enjoying the balance that comes from knowing who you are.

I find myself thinking on Dessaix's prompting during lockdown as well. Even in South Australia, where I am free to drive thousands of kilometres in all directions within the state if I please, I'm most comfortable at home.

Honestly, though, when I have the time to really think about it—which lockdown has allowed in spades—I'm hopeless at doing nothing. As much as I love Dessaix's prompt and I want it to reflect who I am, it's not. Not yet anyway. I read for my job, not just for pleasure, I garden to keep my yard tidy, I do exercise not for the escapism and discipline, but to ward off the sore back I get from sitting at a computer all day, I cook on a Saturday night, an extravagant curry or nasi goreng from scratch and I love it, though when I think about it, I also do it so I can listen to music and drink wine and not feel the need to justify myself. When I think about Dessaix's challenge in the context of Orwell's and Didion's prompts to consider why I write, the time in lockdown has allowed me to reaffirm my love of writing and to remind myself that ultimately, despite the emails, assignments, board minutes, shopping lists and edits I encounter in my everyday life, writing it is something that allows me to make sense of the world and my place within it, just as it did when I would write stories of desert islands and shark attacks when I was a kid.

Time to find inspiration

The pandemic has also presented many opportunities for writers to respond to their experiences, both directly and indirectly, through new creative outputs.

Interestingly, though not altogether unsurprisingly, the story of *Tales from the Decameron*, Boccaccio's 14th-century collection of short stories about a group of seven young women and three young men sheltering together in a villa outside Florence to escape the Black Death resonates once again:

> Some people were of the opinion that living a temperate life, avoiding any kind of excess, was the best protection against the disease. So they formed small communities and lived separately from everyone else, shutting themselves away in houses where there were no sick people and where they could be comfortable. They put themselves on a controlled diet of refined food and quality wines, avoided any kind of overindulgence, allowed no one else to speak with them, refused to hear anything about deaths and sick people in the world outside and spent their time playing music and enjoying such pleasures as they could. Others were drawn to the opposite view. They declared that the most effective medicine when things were as bad as this was to drink a lot, enjoy yourself and go round singing and having fun, doing everything you could to satisfy your urges and desires, and laughing and joking about what was happening.
>
> *(Boccaccio, 2015 [1886], pp.11–12)*

While I'm sure most readers can identify people from both camps during the pandemic, in a contemporary re-thinking of *Tales from the Decameron* for a 21st-century COVID audience, a 'small community' of playwrights in Adelaide, Australia developed their own re-thinking of Boccaccio's text as part of the South Australian State Theatre with 98 performers and 2 theatre companies. The intention of *Decameron 2.0* was to chart the varied responses from the creative sector in Australia, "from a world of complete unknown, to struggling to survive, to developing coping mechanisms, to finding great new things", writes Edwin Kemp Attrill (2020), the artistic director & CEO of ActNow Theatre. Performers presented recorded skits that were broadcast over 10 hours and then re-released via YouTube to be watched by their locked down audience. *Decameron 2.0* explored a plethora of different perspectives around what the pandemic does to people's sense of self, what their plans for the future are and how they reconcile the choices they've made. *Decameron 2.0* featured monologues from a grandmother offering her grandchildren Zoom etiquette tips while remembering the sacrifices made during wartime to contextualise the act of being locked down now; other characters spoke of being aged care workers and following the incessant rules—from washing hands, to keeping distance and wearing masks; other performers detailed how they attended alcoholics anonymous meetings, not for the guidance, but for the company it afforded during lockdown. The *Decameron 2.0* also explored how to balance the uncertainty of being unemployed during lockdown when you've only got $4 left to your name, alongside the difficulty of being a drag queen during a pandemic and the juxtaposition of having and maintaining faith while the world is falling apart.

The inspiration from the *Decameron* was also taken up by the *New York Times Magazine* in 2020 when they enlisted the help of 29 authors to creatively respond to both the *Decameron* and their pandemic experiences.

As the editor Rivka Galchen wrote of the response to both COVID and the original protagonists of the *Tales from the Decameron*:

> They returned not because the plague was over—they had no reason to believe it was. They returned because having laughed and cried and imagined new rules for living altogether, they were then able to finally see the present, and think of the future.
>
> *(Galchen, 2020)*

As an extension of the modern re-thinking of Boccaccio's text, Margaret Attwood wrote a strange parable about alien invaders arriving during the pandemic and caring for the quarantined humans by telling them interpretations of fairy tales to pass the time. Mia Couto wrote a story of a man robbing a COVID positive patient while still maintaining safe distance, and Dinaw Mengestu wrote a short piece on imaginative travel in a D.C. taxi during COVID. The protagonist is taken through Washington by his uncle in a taxi, and in each trip as he turns the meter on, they fill the time and space with information, anecdotes, and facts about an imaginative journey:

> That was how the games we had played in his cab always began, with a flip of the meter and him turning toward the back seat to ask me, "Where would you like to go, sir?" Over the few months we played that game, we never repeated the same place twice. We started local—the Washington Monument, the museums along the Mall—but then quickly expanded to increasingly remote destinations: the Pacific Ocean, Disney World and Disneyland, Mount Rushmore and Yellowstone National Park, and then once I learned more about world history and geography, Egypt and the Great Wall of China, followed by Big Ben and the Colosseum in Rome.
>
> *(Mengestu, 2020)*

Time to re-think

This pause also presents the opportunity to look at how COVID provides the space re-think many creative offerings. I initially approached this book from a travel-centred perspective and the pause in travel writing during the pandemic highlights how we might approach other forms of writing and expression in a more meaningful manner in the future.

Looking at the illness chapter and the validity of the perspectives of Bauby, Bailey and even Henry Lawson, which may have seemed hard to identify with until recently, there is a shared understanding of the experience now and of being isolated and writing about it, which offers the opportunity to explore and celebrate writing and different forms of isolation for what they can teach us about our COVID-19 experience. As Susan Sontag wrote in her *Illness as Metaphor* response to having breast cancer in 1978:

> Everyone … holds dual citizenship, in the kingdom of the well and in the kingdom of the sick. Although we all prefer to use only the good passport, sooner or later each of us is obliged, at least for a spell, to identify ourselves as citizens of that other place.
>
> *(Sontag, 1978, p.3)*

Now with the benefit of perspective from the pandemic we can better understand and value what it is to hold both these passports and how we might utilise them in the future for more diverse and inclusive writing.

Travel writing post-COVID

The prompt for this book came from my own relationship with and inability to travel while exploring the broader concept of how writers throughout history, when faced with different challenges of isolation and confinement, have managed to rediscover their creativity and purpose and through imaginative travel.

Fundamentally, the chapters in this book expand from the first chapter on travel writing to explore how different writers have responded to isolation and confinement and still managed to both travel and to write—to transport themselves and their readers beyond their situations with creativity and purpose. After exploring these different themes, ideas, authors, and scenarios, what can the travel writing genre learn as it emerges post-COVID? For it to continue along a new path, incorporating the valid criticisms of its orientalist and imperialist past, and critiques of its modern reliance on social media and PR, how can it utilise the benefit of the pandemic's pause to re-think what it does in a more meaningful sense?

During the time living through the pandemic and writing this book it has also given me a chance to re-think my place in the genre I have existed within for the past 20 years. When we consider travel writing through the lens of both its problematic past, and now, with its uncertain future, there is a complexity which is worth further consideration. While the pandemic might seem like the event that precipitates the end of travel writing, it also offers a circuit breaker, and a chance to re-think what the genre might do better in the future.

As Paul Fussell writes in *Abroad* (1980), the most notable circuit breaker of the last 100 years for travel writing (before now) was undoubtedly the inter-war period in the 1920s and 1930s. Once the isolation imposed by the First World War was over, travellers and writers who had been isolated at home for years ventured into new places, across newly formed borders and into the world with an enthusiasm for re-discovery. This closer look at the new boundaries of their world meant that travel books also became "a subtle instrument in ethics" (Fussell, 1980, p.204) that allowed "discursions" for this first time, where there was evidence of greater depth and an inner and outer journey in the travel writing of the era as a response to the heroic and imperialist tone of the past.

The most helpful example of how we might employ this post-pandemic re-thinking of travel writing comes from Professor Stephen Muecke's creative and cooperative ethnographies seen as contributions to the re-thinking of travel writing. Muecke's work provides an important consideration for how collaboration with Indigenous writers and migrants can provide a richer and more authentic rendering of place in contemporary Australia. Muecke has done this with *Reading the Country* (1996), written collaboratively with Moroccan artist Krim Benterrak and Indigenous man Paddy Roe, and his own *Gulaga Story* (2007) essay.

In *Reading the Country* Benterrak, Muecke, and Roe demonstrate how a different form of vertical travel allows us to appreciate travelling along the northwest coast of Western Australia. Paddy Roe is a Nyigina man from Roebuck plains, an area once inhabited by Indigenous people, though now it is silent except for the vast cattle studs. Roe identified Muecke's writing and Benterrak's painting and they decided to travel together to compile "poetry of fragmentation, contradiction, unanswered questions, specificity, fluidity and change" (Benterrak, Muecke, & Roe, 1996, p.19). They are drawn together with a combined desire to explore a method for examining the different meanings of place on Roebuck Plains and how different people see and interpret this traveling in place: "the botanist reads the country in terms of its plant life, the tourist in terms of its beauty, and so on" (ibid., p.20). Early Europeans saw it for agricultural possibilities, and hippies for the potential for magic mushroom collection.

Central to the book is the premise that their method is not 'THE' way of interpreting Roebuck plains, their nomadology, as they come to call it is an "archive of fragments" (ibid., p.254) and as much as possible it allows for the country to write itself in a manner that is both novel and important.

Another useful example of how we might better practice and engage with travel writing post-pandemic is Muecke's *Gulaga Story*, which uses a fictocritical approach to write about an ascent of Gulaga, or Mount Dromedary in southern NSW in Australia.

> Travelling whitefellas tend to think in lines, like the roads they eventually build and drive along, like the chronological histories they tell. Yet there are alternatives: being multiply present, for instance, as if by landing up in someone else's somewhere, you still remain somewhere else. Maybe other people have been where you come from too; you arrive in their place and they tell you they have seen your city or your country.
>
> *(Muecke, 2007, p.84)*

Muecke's travel writing combines interviews with anthropologist Debbie Rose and he gets local Yuin Aboriginal people to take him up the mountain to learn aspects of its Dreaming story and the totem of the Yuin. To further demonstrate this multiplicity, Muecke includes sections of Captain Cook's journal when he was travelling along the NSW coast in the 18th century as the initial surface appraisal, before allowing the Yuin to demonstrate the depth and deeper meanings from the Indigenous perspective. While Mount Dromedary might seem like a place with a nice view and a curious name on initial inspection, Muecke presents multiple versions to leave the reader with layers of vertical travel experience, so as to reconsider the depth of meaning that can be appreciated with something that seems as simple as a bush walk up a moderately high mountain.

> Everyone has already been here before you, that's what makes the trip worthwhile, the wearing away of the spot with repeated rubbing, the touching up of the paintings with fresh ochre, once a season, the poetic words repeated in that same place, the dancing that pounds and hardens the earth, and finally, the initiates' flesh cut in that place, and the blood dripping onto the sand.
>
> *(Muecke, 2007, p.84)*

Muecke and his collaborator's travel writing is instructive for its ability to transcend traditional boundaries, and when we consider this in the context of the style of travel writing previously practiced by Karr and de Maistre, as a form of vertical travel, or the consideration of 'from below' history from Darnton (1984) it offers the possibility that an imaginative re-thinking of the form, embracing the collaborative approach of Muecke, along with the vertical travel appreciation of 'place' with traditional owners, recent migrants and containing digressions into cuisine, architecture or music could allow more meaningful and creative engagement not only with Australian travel writing but also with the genre more broadly into the future, where the need to venture far from home is neither as pressing or as possible as it once was post-COVID.

* * *

Travel in the contemporary setting is often linked with tourism and its commodification and cultural and environmental impact, though in the context of this book there is another, more creative consideration. While writing within confinement, as demonstrated in these chapters, does allow for examples of hope, of legacy, and of agency, more importantly it demonstrates the importance of allowing the writer to 'travel' beyond their situation to an imagined home, to appreciate the 'near at hand' in a new way, to a distant family or future lover, into the pages of another's story or, in some cases back to the place of their initial isolation for the freedom and idealism it offered them.

What can we learn from all these themes and examples? How is all this useful to us now having experienced a pandemic? There is so much diversity presented by these writers and their experiences—hardships, difficulties, death, and illness. However, there is also light, and humour within them as well. Anne Frank, despite her horrific final years, is full of optimism and love, Elisabeth Tova Bailey is full of curiosity and affection for her snail, even Xavier de Maistre is compelled by emotion to write in this vertical manner while incarcerated because he hoped and expected it would make some sort of difference outside the confines of his room. What follows is a series of writing prompts, based loosely on the themes of this book, both as techniques I have used for my own writing and as hopeful and helpful activities to start to discover the inspiration from within the idleness of lockdown that Dessaix hopes for. This section utilises the lessons that have been presented from the other writers who have faced their own versions of lockdown, isolation, and confinement, yet they have still found creative ways to express themselves.

Time to write

While there is nothing inherently good about our collective experiences and COVID lockdowns, it does offer the chance for us all to travel, to write and imaginatively transport ourselves into the memories of past adventures, into the 'close' travel stories of the recipes on our kitchen benches we might otherwise ignore, or to step back and appreciate the historical significance of COVID. The opportunity to rethink the imaginative importance of travel has always been available to us, though often, as with so much of life, it is only when our routine is so drastically altered that we take stock of the deeper meanings. As the saying goes, 'this too shall pass', though when people look back on and read about the pandemic in 10 years, or 250, they might be able to better appreciate the multiplicities of travel it allowed if it is written about creatively.

On travel

Seeing as this exploration began with Xavier de Maistre and his room, it is a nice place to begin writing about. *Choose a room that you've gotten to know in greater detail during lockdown*—it could be your bedroom, kitchen, shed or library nook at university. Using a close travelling awareness, write a description of your room. Start with the details that are most obvious: in my home office it is the fluffy carpet under my bare feet, the white windowsill with spider webs at its edges, and the globe I spin during moments of boredom. Show rather than tell the reader what is there. *Then look closer again*. Focus this time on the objects within this room: I look at the painting of a rural field in southern Australia painted by my grandmother, the large, framed photo of the Bagan temples at sunset behind me, and the rock painted with 'I Love U' created by my children as a Father's Day paper weight. *As stage three*, now start to think about the stories of these objects, firstly the origin story: I recall where I bought the Moroccan mirror on my wall from a market in Marrakesh. *Then bring the scene to life*. Write the story of these objects, intersecting and overlapping, use poetry, creative non-fiction or travel writing to bring the space, the memories, and the vertical travel to life in the genre that fits most naturally with your writing. You could try a mixed fictocritical approach blending genres and styles. When I look at the picture of Bagan on my own wall, I remember being in Myanmar 15 years ago by myself. I arrived at the temples after an arduous bus, boat, and train journey from the south wearing thongs and with no plan for the week. I rented a pushbike, and I would cycle aimlessly around the red dirt plains finding abandoned and quiet temples to write in my journal and to take photos. Hot air balloons would float on the horizon at sunset and bullock carts would kick up plumes of ochre dust in the still and muggy evening air. I remember the young boy who found me when I punctured the tyre of my bike and he offered his services as a tour guide, showing me temples, telling stories, and revealing a side of life around Bagan I never would have anticipated. Suddenly I'm not in my office anymore, I'm vertically travelling and I'm remembering the other strands of that same voyage, the spicy noodle soup that tasted of lemon grass I bought on a street corner that evening, the green label on the Myanmar lager and the story I wrote for the *Sydney Morning Herald* about the experience months later. See if you can transport yourself (and your reader) in a similar fashion.

De-familiarising place

Another interesting lockdown writing experiment is around seeing a place with new eyes. I first employed this idea with the 2016 book I wrote *After Dark: A*

Nocturnal Exploration of Madrid where I spent the summer months one year walking the streets of Madrid after dark to discover a different side of the city and to push the boundaries of the genre of writing I was normally so comfortable writing within:

> Just like the night in Madrid, though, many of the walks I took were circuitous and rambling; they would re-cross the same areas and the different times of night would offer different perspectives. Nightwalking in Madrid is as much a temporal phenomenon as it is a spatial activity.
>
> *(Stubbs, 2016a, p.x)*

While I was writing *After Dark*, I often became lost, though as I became more comfortable, I would discover different layers to places I knew well during daylight, and it opened up new story possibilities. I returned to Madrid in early 2019 (mere weeks before COVID locked everything down) to run a series of workshops with a group of NYU students there for a holiday intensive writing course. To get the students into the mindset of the de-familiarisation of place I had employed we set a series of writing activities around their campus and local area in central Madrid. They would travel in pairs and firstly they could only turn left when they felt the need to turn while walking along the street. The next group were given the challenge to buy something in a store they'd never been in. Another group were told to stop at the same bench every day at the same time for a week and capture their observations. From all these exercises the students came up with a set of unique, creative, and interesting renderings of urban Madrid, all different and more tuned into the details around their campus they so often had walked past and ignored. During our own lockdowns these de-familiarisation exercises can also be a wonderful way to 'see' something different and to write something with unexpected layers. Try the turn left trick if it works where you live, find a bench in a nearby park, or go to the Bangladeshi grocery store on the main street to see what 'else' there might be in your local area. Just as with the room exercise, add this to your writing portfolio as you expand the vertical travel perspective of your local area.

On illness

In the chapter on illness and creative writing I looked at examples where writers had used their impairments to focus more deeply on other perspectives and supplementary senses to draw out a new way of experiencing place. In my creative writing classes I do a similar exercise where I get my students to pay more attention to their sensory images: sight, sound, taste, touch and smell. I give them 30 minutes to go out onto campus and to then choose one sense. They are to sit in one spot for the entire time and focus on what is going on around them, though only on the smells, or sounds for example. Groups of students often sit together, though when the writing is segmented like this it produces interesting, and completely different, narratives of the same space.

In your own lockdown environment this can be another interesting way to vertically expand the experience of space. By embodying the experience of the hearing and sight impaired writers and travellers featured in Chapter 3, try to write in the same space, but close your senses off one at a time to see if you can discover the 'skin of the light' as Cixous called it and a different way of accessing somewhere that might seem familiar and ordinary. In an essay I wrote about vision impairment and travel writing previously, I began with this prompt:

> Close your eyes. Wait until the echoes of sunlight fade and the phosphenes floating around your eyeballs dissipate and everything is black. Within this darkness, if you concentrate, you can see through a pea-sized hole of light that will allow you to navigate along an unfamiliar street. This is the reality of many vision-impaired people. The sounds around you are no longer peripheral; the traffic feels closer and more aggressive, people chatter along the street and you grab phrases from the air around you.
>
> *(Stubbs, 2016b, p.128)*

Travelling through food

Food is another way that many people navigate through their traditional travel experiences (the pizza in Napoli, the fresh fruit in the push carts on the streets in Bangkok or the Turkish delight from the markets in Istanbul), and it is also a way that many people have enlivened their lockdown experiences by extending their cooking repertoire. For this exercise, try and include a recipe from your friends or family. Think of something that has a story attached to it that allows you to go into the encounters, the history and the eating of the dish as an extension of close travel.

I asked my wife for help with this exercise (while we were both working from our home offices). She recalled the Sunday lunches she would have every week of her childhood with her parents and grandparents in the Buenos Aires suburb of Wilde. While the meat of Argentina is well known, many families would make Sundays their pasta day, such as this spinach ravioli dish.

Ingredients

Dough

4 eggs
400 grams plain flour
15 ml olive oil

Filling

1 large brown onion
1/2 large red capsicum
400 grams cooked spinach
200 grams ham
1 brain 300 grams (small cow)
50 grams grated parmesan cheese
1 egg
A pinch of salt
Pepper
Nutmeg
Cinnamon
Olive oil

Instructions

1. Put dough ingredients into a blender until the dough is formed. Knead for 5 to 10 minutes. Wrap in clingwrap and let it rise for 30 minutes.
2. Chop the onion and capsicum very finely. Sauté the onion in olive oil and add capsicum. Cook it until it is soft, but not crispy.
3. Remove from heat and add the chopped brains, spinach, ham, and cheese mixture. Season with salt, pepper, nutmeg, and cinnamon.
4. Add the beaten egg and let the mixture cool down.
5. Stretch half the dough quite thin (2mm).
6. Sprinkle the dough and the raviolera (ravioli mould) with flour. Then place the dough in the raviolera. Place spoonfuls of the mixture in each mould until full. Stretch another piece of the dough over the top of the mould and mixture.
7. Now use the rolling pin to cut each ravioli square and discard the leftover pastry. Turn the raviolera upside down to dislodge the squares.
8. In a large saucepan, fill with salted water, and bring it to the boil. Boil a few ravioli at a time so they don't become gluggy (5–8 minutes or until desired consistency is achieved). Do this until the batch is completed and serve with your favourite napolitana sauce.

Beyond this being a traditional Argentinian lunch recipe from the 1990s, it also prompted my wife to recall the details surrounding the meal. They would eat it at her grandmother's house in suburban Buenos Aires, a whitewashed brick home with iron bars across the front windows. Out the back as you walked through the dark and cool house it was full of white flowering May bushes and pink and purple hydrangeas.

The family's most vivid memory of this meal isn't a particularly delicious batch, it is of the taste gone wrong. My wife's grandmother had a special wooden board she'd had for many years to make the ravioli for their Sunday lunch. It had never been washed. Ever. My wife didn't know this as a 10-year-old eager to please, and one Saturday afternoon before the pasta making began, she set to cleaning it with a special wood polishing spray. It wasn't until after the next day's ravioli had been made, with the spinach, the brains, and the whole batch had been cooked and served that everyone realised the pasta now tasted like cedar and bleach. They don't recall ever eating it again.

Writing with others

Write something with your children (or a niece or nephew). It could be a story inspired by a unique lockdown experience such as Mengestu's in the *New York Magazine*, or something based on journal entries. For most of us, this is the most significant world event in recent years, and (hopefully) it will be the most taxing period of our lifetimes. With so much focus on vaccines and saving the adult population though, I think it is sometimes forgotten what the impact is on children.

If you follow this through, for fun, or as a diary of your own pandemic experience, collate all these pieces together so that you can observe, just like the chapters in this book, the different faces and expressions that eventuate when writing behind closed doors.

An interesting addition to this could be the juxtaposition of a similar journal or creative contribution from a relative in the past, whether that is a war journal, a notebook from the Influenza of 1918 or even Facebook messages of travelling and adapting from the previous H1N1 and H5N1 flu strains through Avian and Swine flus in recent years. Do you have a friend or relative who has endured one of the periods of isolation featured in this book? What were their experiences like, and how do they compare to yours now?

A close travel quest

In Robin Hemley's wonderful book *A Field Guide for Immersion Writing* (2012) he bookends his chapters with immersive exercises to fire the imagination and to prompt unexpected writing activities. There is something we can learn from Hemley in this context as well:

> Can you imagine embarking on a quest that doesn't involve travel? A task? A project? A goal or resolution that's always eluded you? The harder the task, the better. And again, it should be something for which you can identify some emotional stakes.
>
> *(Hemley, 2012, p.53)*

Hemley's query is interesting here for how we can think about the value of close travel exercises. It's all well and good to tell the story of the mug on your desk, though if there is emotion attached to it then the story of that object becomes more engaging for both the writer and the reader: you remember the mug came in a set of two from a market in Argentina and your friend, visiting from Turkey, accidentally broke it, though he replaced it with a set of ornate tea glasses in a blue velvet case that you only ever bring out when he visits. And so on. Going through old photos, journals, emails, and even books can fire the same emotional starting points for interesting close travel stories.

Hemley recognises the value of the close travel perspective and how it can allow you to not only look closer at something, but to find a new and unexpected narrative as well. He calls this a "forensic journey" (Hemley, 2012, p.144). Using the inspiration from both de Botton's *A Week at the Airport* (de Botton, 2009), and Hemley's alternative suggestion to "spend a week camped out somewhere we usually avoid, say, a graveyard or in a mall (obviously, the logistics of this are half the battle—getting permission, first of all)" (Hemley, 2012, p.144), see if you can come up with a list of places in your local area (a five kilometre radius to use the COVID confinement measurement) that you either don't know at all, or you pass by often and would like to know more. Then ask yourself why this place has got your attention and start to investigate and write the story.

People

The connection with people has been an enduring theme during lockdown as we've been held apart from many of our friends and family. You can address this somewhat by getting to know the people around you in greater detail. In your local area, assuming you're able to interact with people (through masks of course!) act like a travel writer arriving to a new and exotic place, act like a tourist in a different country within your own street and ask questions of the people around you. What is the cultural background of your neighbour? When did they arrive here (in the street, in the city, in the country)? Ask people who speak different languages about migrant experiences in the place you call home. Ask them questions about where they'd like to travel and why.

What the experience of COVID has taught many of us is the ultimate drudgery and frustration at being locked down. What we can also, hopefully appreciate, is that others have been similarly locked down with much higher stakes, such as Anne Frank, yet they have written interesting, insightful, and valuable accounts of their time in isolation.

Create your own castaway narrative

For the final exercise, we return to one of the most evocative examples of writing and confinement, the story of Robinson Crusoe.

Using your ability to imaginatively travel, if you happened to be on a ship that beached itself on a tropical atoll, or a plane that came down in an isolated reef like the character in *Castaway*, what 10 items would you take with you from the wreckage and why?

From this point you have a decision to make. You're not injured, though you're wet and hungry. You've managed to save your 10 items in a bag on your back; with a mouthful of seawater and pockets full of sand you stumble onto the beach of an island, alone. Which way do you go? Now write the first 24 hours of your time on the island like travel story.

There is a lot we can learn (and hopefully have absorbed) from the trials of Selkirk, de Maistre, Frank, and others. I hope there is also something we've learned from the imaginative possibilities of writing while isolated and confined. I don't think we'll quite reach the sense of calm from Alain de Botton at the end of his Heathrow book, where he realised that with all this close travel awareness he worried that he'd "never have another reason to leave the house" (de Botton, 2009, p.106), though I do think that by reading and reflecting on how others have approached writing and confinement in the past, it can make our own journeys in the future more worthwhile and meaningful if we're able to imaginatively travel beyond our circumstances.

References

Attrill, E (2020). Decameron 2.0. Retrieved from https://statetheatrecompany.com.au/decameron-2-0/.

Benterrak, K, Muecke, S, & Roe, P (1996). *Reading the Country: Introduction to Nomadology*. Fremantle Arts Centre Press.

Boccaccio, G (2015 [1886]). *Tales from the Decameron* (trans. P Hainsworth). Penguin.

Boochani, B (2020). Writing through fences. *The Saturday Paper*, 19–25 September. Retrieved from www.thesaturdaypaper.com.au/culture/books/2020/09/19/writing-through-fences/1600437600010433#hrd (accessed 30 September 2020).

Coat of Hopes (2021). Coat of hopes journey week 7: Crosby Ravensworth–Gretna. Retrieved from www.coatofhopes.uk/pilgrim-gallery-page-07.

Darnton, R (1984). *The Great Cat Massacre and Other Episodes in French Cultural History*. Allen Lane.

de Botton, A (2009). *A Week at the Airport: A Heathrow Diary*. Profile.

Dessaix, R (2017). *The Pleasures of Leisure*. Penguin.

Didion, J (1976). Why I write. *The New York Times*.

Fussell, P (1980). *Abroad: British Literary Traveling between the Wars*. Oxford University Press.

Galchen, R (2020). The Decameron Project: new fiction. *New York Times Magazine*, 7 July. Retrieved from www.nytimes.com/interactive/2020/07/07/magazine/decameron-project-short-story-collection.html.

Gates, C (2020). Word Christchurch book festival sells out despite Covid disruption. Retrieved from www.stuff.co.nz/the-press/news/123211439/word-christchurch-book-festival-sells-out-despite-covid-disruption.

Hemley, R. (2012). *A Field Guide for Immersion Writing: Memoir, Journalism, and Travel*. University of Georgia Press.

Partogi, S & Emilia, A (2020). Online literary festival connection people around the world. *Jakarta Post*, 29 December. Retrieved from https://newgelora.thejakartapost.com/life/2020/12/28/online-literary-festivals-connect-people-around-the-world.html.

Iyer, P (2014). *The Art of Stillness: Adventures in Going Nowhere*. Simon & Schuster.

Marsh, W (2020). 'We dodged a bullet, but of course it circled back around': Literary festivals look beyond lockdown. *The Guardian*, 6 December. Retrieved from www.thegua

rdian.com/culture/2020/dec/06/we-dodged-a-bullet-but-of-course-it-circled-back-a round-literary-festivals-look-beyond-lockdown.

Mengestu, D (2020). How we used to play. *New York Times Magazine*, 7 July. Retrieved from www.nytimes.com/interactive/2020/07/07/magazine/decameron-project-short-story-collec tion.html.

Muecke, S (2007). Gulaga story. *Studies in Travel Writing*, 1(11), 83–91.

O'Connor, N (2021). Publishing during a pandemic: Resilience and change. *Learned Publishing*, 34, 68–70.

Orwell, G (2021 [1946]). *Why I Write*. Renard Press.

Poliakova, E (2021). Self-publishing may be the answer to shakeups in the book world amid COVID-19. *The Conversation*, 26 July. Retrieved from https://theconversation.com/self-p ublishing-may-be-the-answer-to-shakeups-in-the-book-world-amid-covid-19-157098.

Rajan, A (2020). How coronavirus infected publishing. BBC News, 16 April. Retrieved from www.bbc.com/news/entertainment-arts-52299925.

Sartre, J (1958). *No Exit* (trans. P Bowles). French Pub. Corp.

Smart, P. (2020). Publishing during pandemic: Innovation, collaboration, and change. *Learned Publishing*, 33, 194–197.

Sontag, S (1978). *Illness as Metaphor*. Penguin.

Stubbs, B (2016a). *After Dark: A Nocturnal Exploration of Madrid*. Signal Books.

Stubbs, B (2016b). A different view. *Southerly*, 76(2), 128–140.

Sullivan, J (2021). Are authors obliged to write about the pandemic? *The Sydney Morning Herald*, 16 September. Retrieved from www.smh.com.au/culture/books/are-authors-o bliged-to-write-about-the-pandemic-20210909-p58q8x.html.

INDEX

Made in the USA
Las Vegas, NV
30 October 2024

6c9f1661-5bdc-4a90-b3bc-227df0f9a1b6R01